Holocaust to Healing

Closing the Circle

To Zac,
Thank you
for caring!
Love

4/26/14

Holocaust to Healing

Closing the Circle

Kati Preston

Edition One
January 2016

First paperback edition January 2016.

ISBN-10: 1519621248
ISBN-13: 978-1519621245

Printed in the United States of America

This book is printed on acid-free paper.

PHOTOGRAPHIC CREDITS: All of the photographs that appear in the book belong to the author or are from the public domain.

Front cover design by Quin Li Fan.

Final layout and production of this book by Anura Gurugé.

For
the dead who cannot speak.

CONTENTS

Kati Preston
-- The Speaker.

FOREWORD TO
'HOLOCAUST TO HEALING: CLOSING THE CIRCLE'

by:

the author

I am standing on the balcony in Nova Scotia, overlooking Bear River flowing in the gorge below the house. The tide is coming in, rapidly swelling the river. It brings with it a light breeze laden with the smell of the sea. The sun is shining and the wind ruffles my granddaughter's red hair as she sleeps in my arms. She stirs and slowly opens her beautiful turquoise eyes. She smiles for me and touches my face ever so lightly with her baby hand.

My heart is full, close to bursting. Tears pour down my face. I start sobbing uncontrollably—for my father, my family, for the millions of people who have perished. I cry for the people in Rimanoczi Utca where I used to live, the people who departed with their suitcases but left their pets behind with their maids. I cry for the old lady down the street who loved her little dog and for Istvanka, my five-year-old playmate I envied so much because his doting parents had a bronze portrait of him in their living room, for Doctor Balint who saved my life when I was a baby. I cry for what used to be Nagyvarad, my land, and my home—the castle in which I was the fairy princess. I cry for the bomb that fell in our garden, for my mother's tears, for her humiliation and torture. I cry for my father who was caught on the road while attempting to leave the country because he needed to see me, his beloved daughter, one more time. As the tears well, I suddenly feel a great peace, the kind I last felt when I nestled in my father's arms on our balcony, looking up at the stars above, breathing in his scent, his love, and his strength. It is as if he has come back to me to make it all good again, to restore me to my palace and my peace. I am full of awe, sorrow, love, and above all, peace—a peace I have not felt since I was a child.

My father was murdered in Auschwitz for being a Jew, but the tiny child in my arms is also the grandchild of a German soldier in the Wermacht. He too had been a victim, so young to be cast into such a role, which he barely understood. Out of all that horror and hell that was the war and the Holocaust, this beautiful child was sent to us, to heal, give me peace and close the circle. I am still sobbing uncontrollably, sobbing because my heart is about to burst with all the fierce, primal love I have for this miraculous life, this child in my arms.

AN INTRODUCTION FOR MY
GRANDDAUGHTERS

Dear girls,

Everybody carries a book inside them, just like every family has a story to tell. If you live long enough and wait to share your story, you will find that it has become far more interesting and will have assumed more and more superimposed layers. Experience is laid upon experience, until our whole character is affected by what has gone before.

We are all of a long line of genes—inherited traits, both physical and emotional. These acquired instincts and atavistic behaviors are passed down in a collective memory. When you see the Canada geese fly south you realize they know to do this because their ancestors passed down their memory in their genes so that later generations of birds could survive. You too have collective memory imprinted in your genes that will help you survive and navigate in the future.

It took me seventy years to realize my purpose in life. It is to do all I can for you to survive—you girls are my zenith and my triumph. You are my genetic success story, the reason and purpose of my survival, my reason for being. In addition to all this, I will try to add what I have learned of our family history—from my own experiences and from the stories told to me by long dead members of our tribe—so that you will know where you come from. You need to know where you come from before you can go anywhere. Where you'll go from here is entirely up to you and knowing who you are might help shape who you can become.

I started this book twice before. My initial undertaking was in my early self-important twenties. But I soon realized I had to live some before I could write about life. During my second attempt, about ten years ago, I had a synopsis and a first chapter and then the computer crashed. So here I am for the third time. Now that I am over seventy I feel have lived long enough to have some experience to pass down to you. Age provides us with many gifts, one being that we can be totally honest and not give a shit what people will think of you. I will be sometimes brutally honest. This is not a pretty fairy story—neither is it all nice. I want to tell the truth, warts and all. I hope it will be valuable to you in the future and that you, in turn, will pass it down to your children, whom I will never know. Remember that my love for you will pass down to them. I will put photographs where they belong in the stories and recipes too, although my next book will be the cookbook you've all requested.

A Thumbnail Sketch of Transylvania

The first chapter of this book, pivotal as it is, is set in Transylvania. What most people (especially in America) know of Transylvania relates to vampires and Count Dracula – and the two *'Hotel Transylvania'* movies have certainly helped in reinforcing this imagery. Count Dracula, brought to life in an 1897 book by Irish author Bram Stoker, is actually based on a real 15th century ruler of the area, Vlad (Drăculea) III, Prince of Wallachia. According to legend the ruthless prince is said to have murdered upwards of 80,000 of his enemies by skewering them on long wooden spikes! There are, however, no vampires stories in this book.

Today's Transylvania is a picturesque, castle-studded region in Central Romania surrounded by imposing mountain ranges – the Carpathian mountain range forming its Eastern boundary. Transylvania, in the crossroad of eastern Europe has a long distinguished history dating back to the Roman Empire – albeit much of it rather exotic, convoluted and complex.

During the time period dealt with in Chapter I some parts of Transylvania were under Hungarian rule. Following World War II the Allies ceded that territory back to Romania.

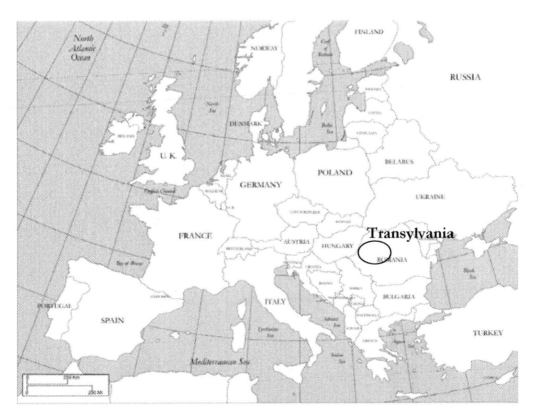

The ghetto in Nagyvarad held 35,000 Jews from the town and the surrounding area of the county of Bihar. This ghetto was completely liquidated between May 23rd and June 27th, 1944. A total of 27,215 Jews including my family were sent to Auschwitz, the rest to Mauthausen. All this was achieved at the very end of the War with the enthusiastic help of the Hungarians, who were keen to be rid of the Jews.

I.
NAGYVARAD

"Kati! Hol vagy? Gyere ide kész a palacsinta." It was grandmama's voice calling, *"Kati, where are you? Come here, your pancake is ready."* I love grandmama's pancakes. She makes them thin, filled with grated walnuts and sugar. She always makes them for me when my governess has her day off. Freulein doesn't let me have pancakes because she wants me to eat "healthy" food like porridge or dumplings, the kind of heavy dumplings that hit the bottom of your stomach when you swallow them. I hate dumplings and I hate Freulein. She has such a sour disposition and an air of constant disapproval. Her lips, which are thin to begin with, disappear in a sneer when she scolds me for some minor transgression or inappropriate behavior.

Mami and Papa think it is a wonderful idea to have a German governess who will teach me all the right things a well brought up young lady needs to know. Oh yes, she teaches me a lot. I can speak and read German fluently and I am only four and a half. I curtsy prettily and sleep in paper curlers so my hair looks perfect in the morning. Freulein believes that to wash in cold water is somehow character building, and that a child should only speak when spoken to. I am not allowed to shout, speak loudly, or skip, and, of course, sliding down the banister is the ultimate form of wickedness. Bedtime is strictly adhered to, and bedtime stories are short and instructive. Her favorite fairy stories are the Grimm Brothers'—nasty tales where a child who sucks his thumb has it cut off with large scissors, or where a little girl goes up in flames because she plays with forbidden matches. When going for a walk, I have to hold my breath when near garbage, beggars, or horse manure on the road. I always wear white spats and never, never go out without gloves or a hat. The worst sin anyone can commit is to eat on the street. I gaze longingly at children eating chestnuts and sweets and playing in the street as Freulein pulls me along with a black gloved hand. I am only allowed to play with children who have governesses or rich mothers. We cannot play just anywhere, but must be escorted to an appropriate venue. There are afternoon teas at each other's houses or, on rare occasion, we meet at the *"Cukraszda,"* the pastry restaurant at the elegant Panonia Hotel. Birthday parties with the right children are also approved, and on these occasions I wear velvet dresses with lace collars, white stockings, and patent leather shoes. I am taken to dance school and a piano teacher comes to the house twice a week. All these activities are always supervised by Freulein. Every morning I am taken to greet my parents at breakfast. At night, if they are home, they come to kiss me good night.

Obedience is contrary to my genetic makeup. I still find I get defiant when commanded to do something without an explanation. Freulein stirs in my young mind a seething resentment to authority. My parents both work very long hours, and go out a lot. It is quite acceptable to let a governess have great control. Perhaps, because both my parents grew up very poor, they are somewhat awed by Freulein who came from some impoverished minor Austrian nobility. Some afternoons Freulein takes me to a dentist where I have to stay in the waiting room with a book. She has very long "treatments." I never complain about Freulein because I am told she does everything for my own good, and I am fortunate to be in such good hands.

Grand-mama is the only one who dared cross Freulein, but she only comes on days she is not there. Grand-mama lives with my Aunt Aranka and her husband. On those days I don't wash my hands because Grand-mama doesn't see any germs when she examines my palm. She believes that if she cannot see something it doesn't exist—except, of course, God, Jesus, and a whole panoply of assorted saints. On Sundays, when Freulein is off, Grand-mama drags me to Mass at the local church where she prays loudly for my mother's soul because she married a

Jew. I was four when she took me to see the crèche at the church at Christmas. I stole baby Jesus and hid him under my coat. When we got home I was rushed back to Church and was told off by a very stern priest.

Out apartment is on the first floor of a very spacious house. You can see the park and river from the windows. We are the only tenants because my mother has her dressmaking business in part of the house. There is a front staircase and a back one used by the seamstresses, the servants, and tradesmen. I love the back staircase because it has a great banister to slide on, and I am not really supposed to be there. The back of the apartment overlooks a yard with some trees and a big wooden structure used by the maids to beat dust from the Persian rugs. Grand-mama lets me hang on the wooden structure, upside down like a bat.

Our rooms are very large, with high ceilings and beautiful inlaid parquet floors. The floors are constantly shined and polished by assorted maids wearing special foot covers made of soft cloth. In the winter, the rooms are heated by ornate ceramic stoves that stand in a corner of each room. As winters are very cold, all the houses have double sets of windows and roll down shades to keep the cold or the sun out, depending on the season. In winter, I go sledding in the park or go on walks in town to look at the Christmas decorations in the shop windows. It gets dark early, and there are pretty lights everywhere. There is a smell of roasting chestnuts in the air and I feel happy and excited.

In the summer it gets very hot for days on end. The greatest treat is going to the swimming pool with Papa. He can swim like a fish. I ride on his back in the water pretending to be a mermaid. These are the happiest moments of my life. The very last photo I have of my father was taken at the swimming pool. I was jokingly putting ears on him.

My room has pale pink silk wall coverings, embroidered with little bunches of flowers. The furniture is also pink with silver edges and decorations. There are white lace curtains on the tall windows that billow like sails when the wind blows. I imagine I am a fairy princess on a sailing ship. In bed, I wait for my parents to come to say goodnight. Most nights it is Freulein who comes to my room. She never kisses me but tells me to go to sleep and be quiet. I sneak out and climb into my parents' bed and bury my face in their pillows. I can smell my mother's perfume and my father's aftershave and tobacco. I feel so safe there.

I have trouble falling asleep. I have a nightmare and call for my mother. Freulein comes into the room wearing black gloves and waves her hands in front of my face like claws, threatening me to make me stop crying. My mother, who had gone out earlier, comes home because she forgot something. As she comes to check on me she finds me cowering in a corner of my bed while Freulein waves her gloved "claws" in my face. My mother always had an explosive temper and

Freulein is dismissed then and there. I watch her suitcases flying out the window onto the sidewalk where a carriage is waiting to take her to the train station. I am happy she is gone and don't feel sorry for her.

My life changes after Freulein leaves. I am sent to the Jewish Kindergarten. There are boys and girls I already know, but to my great delight Istvanka is there too. Istvanka is a little boy, my neighbor. His family dotes on him—the only child of a doctor and his beautiful wife. They have portraits of him all over their house. But what I admire and envy most is a plaster bust of his head prominently displayed on a shelf. Istvanka is my love. I chase him around and plant kisses on his cheeks, which he rubs off with his sleeves. He likes to play running up and down the circular drive in front of the Opera near our street. We could never do this when Freulein was in charge, but now we play there a lot.

In Kindergarten we play and sing. We are taught all about various Jewish holidays, which are all new to me. During Hanukkah we play with a deridle and light candles.

I was born here in 1939, not an auspicious time in Europe to have a child, but as my parents were aged forty and thirty, they wanted a child before they got older. I was very much a wanted love child.

Nagyvarad is a town in a region called Transylvania, which today is in Romania. It was in Romania when I was born and then the Germans gave it to Hungary. It was mainly the Hungarians who exterminated us with such zeal and enthusiasm. Nagyvarad had a large Jewish population. There were several synagogues, a Jewish hospital, Jewish Kindergarten, Jewish school. Nagyvarad had a varied and vibrant cultural life. There was the Opera and several theatres. After Freulein left and I was sent to the Jewish Kindergarten, there were fifty-two children there. After the war, only two of us were left.

I don't remember it ever raining in Nagyvarad until the war came. Even then it only rained to put out the fires the bombs left in their wake. Dealing with memories is like working a jigsaw puzzle. We remember fragments that eventually coalesce to form vivid pictures in our minds though many of the pieces of the puzzle are missing

My Parents

entirely. I was a sickly child, but have no memory of it. I only know the stories my mother told me about it. My pediatrician Dr. Balint saved my life when he used an innovative technique, which involved the removal of a piece of diseased bone behind my ear. During the Holocaust, Dr. Balint and his whole family were exterminated in Auschwitz.

Happy one-year-old with father Ernest

Aged one with mother Gabriella

It is night in my room. I had been asleep a long time. Mother and Father are in my room, returning from a party and coming to check on me and kiss me good night. They are young, vibrant, handsome, and elegant. I smell mother's perfume and father's smell of cologne and tobacco. I feel so safe, enveloped in a cocoon of love as I drift off to sleep again.

I am having a nightmare. I am screaming. The door opens and Papa scoops me up in his arms and takes me to their bed. I lie on my back, snuggled between my parents. We are all three connected. I am safe now and drift off to sleep.

Of course it is always warm and sunny in my little world. In our street, the older children must all learn to play the piano. Up and down the street it is all Chopin etudes or Beethoven's "Für Elise," played more or less badly. All the children in our street have beautiful clean clothes and shiny hair. The little girls are made to sleep in paper curlers and wear bows during the day. When attending parties at one another's houses, we wear white stockings, patent leather shoes, and velvet dresses with lace collars.

I was an only child, born to Gabriella, aged 30, and Ernest, aged 40. I am very special because before me they had twin boys and a little girl. All three were born prematurely and didn't survive. I lived like a little princess—loved, spoiled, and indulged by all. Perhaps it was this totally unconditional adoration that gave me strength to battle life later on. You can spoil a child, but life has a brutal way of unspoiling you.

When I was born, my parents were, for those times, considered very well off. My mother had a dressmaking business employing forty seamstresses. She was very popular and people came to her from many surrounding towns to have their dresses designed and made by her. There was a large religious Jewish community in Nagyvarad and the surrounding towns and my mother made their wedding dresses. These were modest, beautiful gowns with high necks and long sleeves that covered part of their hands. She traveled to Paris twice every year and had a photographic memory for the new styles she saw there. In the evenings after the fashion shows, she would sketch every detail of every garment. She would then return home, inspired by the new Paris styles and turn out beautiful, stylish dresses.

My father had a wholesale freshwater fish business. It supplied the whole area with fresh fish from the hatcheries he owned on the river Koros, which ran through our town. Frequently, there were carp swimming in our bath to stay fresh until the cook prepared them for dinner. I used to think the carp looked like old peasants with long moustaches swimming to and fro in the bath. We had a cook, Freulein the governess, two housemaids, and a kitchen maid. Nobody had cars and taxis were horse drawn carriages. The coachman sat up front and there were two benches like seats facing each other for the passengers. There was a large folding canopy cover in the event of rain or too much sun. In those days in Nagyvarad, if you were somebody, your children were educated by a German or Austrian governess—at least for families who spoke Hungarian. The ethnic Romanians had

Gabriella and Ernest in Venice, 1938

French governesses. They leaned toward the French and not the Austro-Hungarian culture. After German Jews, Hungarian Jews were the most assimilated in Europe; they loved their country, culture, and language. Feeling Hungarian, they blossomed in all aspects of life. These educated, cultured Jews dominated most of Hungarian culture. They were in the vanguard of literature, theatre, film, and music, and, of course, the professions of law, science, and medicine. In fact, later Hollywood and the whole movie industry was started by Hungarian Jews. In the early years, there used to be a big sign in a Hollywood studio reception area that said, "It is not enough to be Hungarian, you also need talent."

My parents traveled abroad often, which was very unusual in those days. I was made in Venice. My parents were in Italy and I was conceived there.

Ernest and Gabriella in
Piazza St. Marco

To this day, I think Venice is a magical place, one of the incredible artistic human achievements. I have since been back many times and walked the piazzas and sidewalks trying to capture some remote feeling of my parents fleeting youth, life, love, and happiness there.

Whenever I am in Venice, I walk along the canals and take the bridges that connect the town. It is magical to walk on cobblestones worn shiny by generations for hundreds of years. I feel the stones remember and absorb the memories of generations. I keep touching the stone balustrades on the bridges, trying to connect with my parents in some subliminal way. They say that buildings absorb violence and evil from the past and create certain vibes that some people are sensitive to. I wonder if love, passion, and happiness can leave an imprint too. They were happiest there, in the sun, in Venice. Life was good, and they were young and so very much in love. If there is life after death, they would be there in Venice. It would be their paradise. I close my eyes. I so want to feel their presence.

My parents were both born very poor. My mother's mother Juliana was a staunch Hungarian Catholic who married beneath her. Her husband, my grandfather, was Teodor Botzoc, a Greek Orthodox Romanian peasant. It was a marriage based on passion, which soon turned to hatred. They fought like cats and dogs until my mother persuaded them to divorce when she was sixteen. Juliana in her youth was a pretty woman with beautiful gray eyes and luxurious light brown wavy hair. She was tall and imperious and refused to live in the village because she felt it was beneath her to be a peasant's wife. So they became caretakers for a large apartment block and lived in a tiny apartment in the courtyard. Money was very tight. The economy was bad and there were no other jobs. Four children were born in quick succession.

Gabriella was the Juliana's eldest. When she was three Juliana gave birth to stillborn baby on her own without medical attention. Teodor was at his family farm when the baby came. Depleted by the birth, Juliana fell into an exhausted sleep and the neighbors found three-year-old Gabriella playing in the yard with the dead baby. She finally had a baby doll like the rich children, and cried bitterly when the baby was taken away from her. Two more girls were born later, Aranka and Bozsi.

Eventually my Grandfather Teodor managed to get a job on the railway and worked his way up to become a driver. While the girls were growing up the parents fought incessantly and sometimes violently. Teodor would smack Juliana around if the food was not crisp enough. He liked it a little burnt. Juliana would smack him around when he would come home drunk, smelling of strange women. Both being good-looking people, poor and unhappily married, sought solace in drink, sex, and flirtations. Once Juliana came home unexpectedly and found Teodor in bed with three women. She poured a kettle of hot water on them. Juliana called Teodor a filthy Rumanian peasant and he, in turn, called her a Hungarian whore. These shenanigans continued until finally they got divorced.

Because of an untreated early childhood illness my mother Gabriella couldn't hear properly until she was twelve. This of course made school very difficult for the little girl. She hated school. At age of seven, she stole a large slab of bacon and rubbed it all over the outside of the school's walls in the hope the dogs would devour the building. She got into trouble instead for wasting precious food.

Gabriella's best friend was Pista, who lived in a luxury apartment. He was the son of the rich man who owned the apartment building. He was very kind to my mother and always brought her food and little luxuries. He was a gentle boy. Later during

Pista in Italy after the war

the war, Pista, who was a Jew, was deported. Miraculously he survived, but when he was at the railway station to come home, the Russians were missing a prisoner from one of their transports. They caught Pista and took him to Siberia. He survived that too, but when he finally came back the communists deported him to work in some mine because he was gay and therefore an undesirable. We met up with him in New York many years later, he and my mother remained friends until his death. He was such a refined old gentleman.

At the age of twelve Gabriella started work as a dressmaker's apprentice. It was a miserable existence for the scrawny little girl whose main job was to keep the heavy irons burning hot. She would swing the heavy iron back and forth to keep the charcoal inside hot. They would play tricks on her and send her to the shops to buy polka dot sewing thread and have a good laugh at her expense. She worked nine hours a day, six days a week, and didn't learn anything. However, she did get very angry and ambitious and swore she would never work for anyone again. After work, she would go home and make clothes for her sisters with any fabrics she could find. She would cut up curtains, tablecloths, and sew the dresses by hand. At fourteen she advertised herself in a newspaper and started going to people's houses to mend linens and eventually make garments. In those times everything was homemade from bolts of cloth. There were no ready-made garments.

Last photo of Grandfather Teodor and I

Gabriella's confidence grew, and she was more and more adventurous in her work. She got quite a following. She started to realize that every husband and wife didn't hate and smack each other, and that people ate around a table in a civilized manner. She even worked in a house where the family didn't speak to each other—they only communicated by singing Operatic arias superimposing mundane things such as *"Dinner is ready"* or *"Is it raining?"*

Mother grew into a pretty young woman and had many suitors. One in particular pursued her relentlessly, but she was not interested. He was broken hearted and was found hanging in her parents' woodshed.

By the time Gabriella was sixteen she saved up enough money to buy a sewing machine, left home, rented a room, and set up her business. But before she left, she dragged her parents off to get divorced. Juliana moved in with an old boyfriend Joska Bacsi, and Teodor moved in with a Romanian gypsy named Eva. They both seemed to have found some peace at last. The two younger girls stayed with their mother and Gabriella was out on her own.

By this time, Teodor was head driver on the railway and remained in the job until 1940. On the morning he died, Teodor told Eva about a dream he had the night before. He and a group of people were all walking up a hill towards God, who was waiting for them. At noon there was an accident and the train went off a bridge. Eva died a year later from a broken heart.

It was hard to live as a single woman so Gabriella married a lay-about called Feri who took advantage of her. Their ground floor room looked out onto a narrow courtyard with a brick wall. Gabriella painted the bricks white and planted flowers at the base of the wall. One day she caught Feri urinating on her flowers. An argument ensued, Feri hit her, and she blew up. She broke two chairs on him and then went and got the ambulance to take him away. She'd had enough!

When Gabriella met and married Ernest Rubin she was twenty, well established in her business, independent, elegant, and successful. He was ten years older. She converted to Judaism—it was the only way a Jew, like Ernest, could marry outside the faith in those days. His mother was very accepting and kind for those times. His Jewish mother became the mother Gabriella always wanted. They were very close.

My father's parents were both from a small village in Russia. During a pogrom they lost their own parents and families.

The soldiers rode in from the East just as the sun was setting. By the time they left, as night fell, there was very little left of the Jewish village. There was total silence. Only the crackling of the burning wooden structures could be heard. Some houses still stood, but most were in flames. There were no living persons to be seen anywhere. Even the dogs that hadn't run away were slaughtered. The men and women lay dead, some still clutching each other. Others still held onto their children in an attempt to shield them or lay next to sticks and knives—pathetic attempts at defending themselves.

In one of the back rooms, a toddler covered in blood was trying to nurse from the exposed breast of his dead mother. Her dress was up around her hips exposing her torn undergarments. The woman's throat had been slashed. The little boy was hungry and started to cry. A little girl peered out of a shed. Her father had hidden her when he heard the soldiers coming. She came out and sat next to her papa who was still breathing as the last of his blood slowly drained away.

Some Jews who had escaped from another village were hiding in the woods. They heard the little boy cry and found the two toddlers in their burnt out homes. The children were brought to Nagyvarad where the Jewish community provided for them till they grew up and married. Grandpa Rubin's father had been the Rabbi of the village they ransacked. He was the first person killed by the drunken Cossacks.

Grandma Rozsi was very intelligent as well as beautiful. She was tall, slim, and dark, with flashing eyes and a temper to match. Grandpa Rubin, like all Jewish men, could read and was educated, but had no money and earned his living fishing on the river Koros. They were both poor and their union was a logical arrangement among people of similar backgrounds. She had no parents and no dowry, but they seemed to get along. Children followed in quick succession, nine altogether, with two sets of twins. One set was my father Erno and his identical twin brother Shmuel. The eldest girl was ten and the youngest girl was three when the ice gave way under Grandpa one winter day. He fell into the icy water. He managed to climb onto the riverbank but walking home in the freezing weather, got pneumonia, and died a week later.

Rozsi was left in total poverty with nine children to bring up. She borrowed money and bought a market stall where she sold the fish she bought wholesale. Although illiterate, she could calculate in her head and managed to earn enough to feed her children. In the evenings, after the market closed, she would go home and wash all her children's clothes every night. Then she would dry them by the fire and iron them dry for the morning. All her children went to school, and though they only had one set of clothes, they were always spotless. Life was very hard for Rozsi. Her children were always slightly hungry and luxuries such as pastries and cream were out of reach.

All of my father's family documents and photographs were destroyed during the war.

My father Erno, always the resourceful one, would buy a bun and hollow it out by eating the soft bread. He would then go to a stall and ask to buy cream. Not having a container to put the cream in, he would have them pour it into the hollowed bun. Then, after digging around in his pocket and not finding any money, he would have to pour the cream back into the vat and run for his life. A lot of the cream would saturate the bread and then Erno and his brothers would make a meal of the delicious cream soaked crust.

One night after the market closed, it was raining, and in the dark Rozsi roamed the deserted muddy marketplace looking for discarded vegetables to take home to make soup for the children. A devout religious woman, she cried out to God to help her. She was so very tired. Suddenly her foot slipped on something. It was a roll of gold Napoleon coins, a real fortune. She went to ask the Rabbi for advice. He told her to keep the money. This eased her lot and the money enabled her to keep her family for a long time.

Grandma Rozsi Rubin died of diabetes two years before the war broke out. This was a blessing in disguise. She died surrounded by her loving family who by this time numbered twenty-eight souls. She died happy, respected, and loved by all. After the battles to provide for her children she didn't deserve to see them and their beloved families murdered.

We seem to be a family of very strong women for several generations. Women seem to do better in adversity than men. Perhaps we were born to nurture and protect the weaker ones, the children.

Life is wonderful in my world. My father comes home from work and scoops me up in his arms. He kisses me and throws his head back laughing. He has a huge laugh and great capacity for joy. I touch the white silk scarf he always wears when going out, his scent is a mixture of tobacco and cologne. He is dark and has beautiful white teeth. When he takes me swimming in the river, I am never afraid because I am with him. I ride on his shoulders in the water while he swims faster and faster. At night he sometimes reads me a story. Often I sit on his lap on the balcony breathing in the scent of lilacs blooming nearby, while he teaches me the names of all the stars. He is the most important person in my life. I don't love anyone as much.

Walking with Parents on Main Street

It is summer. The stars are bright. Father is holding me on his lap on the balcony, talking to me softly. I am chewing on my gold chain, and feel it snap between my teeth. He doesn't get angry. He simply takes the chain out of my mouth and puts it in his pocket. A few days later the chain is back, repaired.

Mother, father, and I are walking along *Fo Utca*, the Main Street, on Sunday afternoon. I am in the middle, each of them holding one of my hands. My parents are young, elegant and glamorous. I feel happy, safe, and very proud. They stop and chat to lots of people, who smile and pat me on the head.

This is what everyone does on Sundays. People put on their best clothes and walk up and down Main Street, to see and to be seen.

It is Friday night and mother lights candles, covers her head, and prays silently moving her hands before her face. I think she is doing magic. I believe she has magical powers.

Every year we have a huge Christmas tree. My parents do not follow any religion seriously, but they don't not want to deprive me of all the excitement. The tree reaches the tall ceiling and had a beautiful angel on top. It is decorated with shiny balls, ornaments, and lots of homemade candies wrapped in tissue paper with a band of silver or gold paper. It is called *"szaloncukor"* and has an evanescent fruity sweetness, as it melts in my mouth. There are candles on the tree, real candles in little round metal holders clipped to the branches. Every Christmas, the tree catches fire and has to be doused with a bucket of water that always stands nearby. Under the tree are the most beautiful toys to gladden the heart of a much-loved spoiled little girl.

It is Christmas and I am sitting under the tree opening presents. It seems all the gifts are things I already had before. I cry because I really wanted a puppy. The last box seems to move about. I open it and a find a fluffy white kitten inside. I hug the kitten and squeal with joy. *"Lily"* I say. *"I am going to call her Lily!"*

Mother is always standing behind the cutting table in her atelier cutting rhythmically with her great big scissors. She works very hard to keep forty seamstresses busy. When there are customers in the waiting room, my governess parades me around to show off my beautiful dresses and my perfectly curled hair.

My father always gives me some coins when we go on walks and he tells me to give it to beggars. He says that if someone needs to beg it is my duty to help.

Mother at Work

The first sign that things are going wrong is a lot of crying. My mother's Jewish seamstresses cry and my mother cries often too. There is talk of people hating Jews. I have a vague idea I am Jewish, whatever that means. A law comes that all Jews have to wear a yellow star. Mother makes me a beautiful shiny star out of a material that looks like gold. She sews it on my little blue coat and we go out to buy ice cream. I am very proud of my star.

We are walking, my mother holding my hand. A man comes opposite us on the street, stops, looks at me strangely and spits in my face. The spit is running down my cheek. I am shocked because I cannot understand how the man could hate such a beautiful

Last picture with Father

star. Mother just wipes my face. Why does she say nothing?

My father has to report to work detail and leaves town with all able-bodied Jewish men to go build roads for the state. The expression "Budos Zsido" (stinking Jew) becomes more and more common. Our cook leaves and so do the maids and some of my mother's seamstresses. They don't want to work for Jews. Then people just start not being around. All Jews are ordered to report to the "Ghetto."

They build a tall brick wall around a Jewish area and all Jews are supposed to live there. My mother decides that if my father is baptized he might become exempt.

I am not supposed to be in the room but I sneak in and hide behind a large armchair. Father is kneeling in front of a man in a costume (I later realize it was a priest). The man makes my father repeat things after him and then pours some water on his head. The tears are running down my father's face. I want to hug him, to make him feel better, but I have to stay in my hiding place.

Converting doesn't help, so mother organizes documents that would enable my father to go to Romania, where they are not rounding up the Jews. He refuses to leave because he feels his family in the Ghetto needs him, as he is the strongest and most resourceful among them. He believes they are being relocated to work somewhere. They will need his help.

The day my father leaves for the Ghetto is very sad.

I find my parents in the workroom very early in the morning. Father seems to be going on a trip. He has a suitcase next to him. They are standing by the cutting table holding each other and crying. I feel left out. I climb onto the table and worm my way between them. We are now all hugging and they are crying harder. I cry too.

I never saw my father again.

There is no more kindergarten. All the teachers and most of the children are in the Ghetto. The word "Ghetto" is "foundry" in Italian. It was in the foundry area in Venice where the Jews were first interned in the Middle- Ages. It was during this time that Jews had to wear yellow hats and were not allowed out of the Ghetto after dark. This inspired the yellow star.

There are a lot of poor abandoned dogs running around. People are rounded up too fast to give their pets to someone. We take in some dogs and it upsets me to hear the rest of them howling for their masters. This I can understand far more than people being taken away. I weep for the poor dogs, but soon the dogcatcher comes and they are all gone.

My mother assumes that because she is Catholic, I do not have to be sent to the Ghetto. Somehow nobody noticed I am still at home, not until one of her workers tells the authorities. Just as my mother is looking for somewhere to hide me a woman named Erzsebet arrives. Erzsebet had been an orphan who used to deliver our milk. When she got married Mother made her a beautiful wedding dress as a gift. She never forgot this and when she heard they were rounding up the Jews she comes to see us. "I will save your child," she says and I hop onto the seat next to her on her horse drawn wagon. I can't understand why my mother is so distraught. After all, I am going on a great adventure to the country.

Erzsebet's farm is about half an hour away on the outskirts of a small village. The house and the barn face each other in the courtyard. There is a fence on the roadside with a gate through which she drives to the barn. Behind the house and barn is a steep hill covered in grapevines. The barn is not very large. The ground floor has two stalls, one for the cow and one for the horse. The floor above it has a pitched roof, sloping on the sides, with a trap door opening over the entrance below. The barn is full of loose hay, which she throws with a pitchfork down the trap door that has some rickety stairs. She takes me up these stairs and explains that I am only allowed out when she comes for me because if anyone finds out I am here they will come and kill me!

Erzsebet tells me to stay in the barn, but I am afraid of the dark. There are some blankets where the roof slopes so I curl up there and cry. I cry for my father, cry for my mother, and cry because I don't want people to come and kill me. I wonder if someone kills me will I be able to get un-killed? I cry myself to sleep.

When I wake up in the morning it is bright and sunny and I realize that a big mulberry tree laden with fruit has a branch reaching into the barn. Those berries taste so wonderful.

Erzsebet is a widow with a twelve-year-old retarded son. Ocsi has my mental age and so he becomes my only friend and playmate. He is allowed to sneak up to the loft to bring me my meals but I never let him empty my potty—I am too ashamed. Ocsi gives me a small comb for my hair. At one time it had five sparkling stones. Now it is down to one. I cherish this comb for years. I like the smell of the barn, and to this day when I smell hay it makes me feel very safe and calm.

Ocsi and I play doctors and examine each other's bodies. Sometimes Ocsi's "treatments" hurt me but I get over it. He is my friend and doesn't hurt me on purpose. He is kind and cares. He keeps me company and cheers me up when I cry.

It is early morning. There is a lot of commotion in the yard. I peek through a crack and see some men in uniforms with black rooster feathers on their hats yelling at Erzsebet. They have guns with bayonets and come pounding up the barn stairs. I do what Erzsebet taught me and make myself very small, curled up under the hay in a corner where the roof joins the attic floor. The men keep stabbing the hay with their bayonets. One lands near my head. I can hear the "twang" it makes as it hits the wood. They eventually go away. I am terrified, trembling, and can't understand why they want to kill me. I am a good girl.

These were the wonderful collaborators, the Hungarian gendarmes who hunted Jews with such enthusiasm.

Occasionally, I am allowed downstairs into the courtyard to play with the dog and the cat. I cut my finger on an axe and Erzsebet plunges my hand in the dog's water dish to stop the bleeding. I still have the scar. I miss my parents and my home, and cry myself to sleep every night. Some nights Ocsi sleeps in the barn with me.

I later realized that he had molested me sexually. I vaguely remember him doing strange things to me, things that sometimes hurt, but he was, after all, my best and only friend. He was kind and always brought me food to eat or a kitten to play with. Perhaps because of his low IQ, it was more like playing.

About once a week Mother comes at night and visits me at the farm. She has to be very careful because she can put us all in danger. She brings me sweets, toys, and colored pencils. I always cry bitterly when she leaves. I keep asking her when Papa will come. She shakes her head and has tears in her eyes.

One evening as she is leaving her house, one of her workers sees some toys in the basket she is carrying. Like the dutiful collaborator she is, she promptly reports this to the police. I have always despised the sort of person who blindly and unquestioningly follows, or even—to use a stronger term—worships authority. These are the weak people who will never stand up for what is right but will fall in line with rest of the dumb sheep. They are the collaborators, the people who never question authority because they feel weak and insignificant. They follow the bully because they feel some of the power rubbing off on them. They are the people who stood by during every genocide throughout history. As far as I am concerned, not try to do good, is only somewhat less of a sin than actively doing harm. People can do terrible harm by not speaking up.

They are waiting for Mother when she returns home. They arrest her and take her away to the main police headquarters where she is tortured. She never tells them where I am hidden and she never tells me what they did to her. All she says that it was very humiliating, and it would do me no good to know. She eventually buys her way out of there with some gold coins. Gold Napoleons to the rescue once again.

Now they are watching her all the time. Every night someone daubs "Whore of the Jews" on the front door downstairs and my mother cleans it before the start of work. All the Jews being in the Ghetto, her business shrinks and she has much less work. She cannot fire the informant. She is too frightened to.

Rumors start about Jews being sent not to be relocated, but to die. They start transports daily by the trainload. My mother visits my aunt Aranka and her husband Ferenc. They live on the outskirts of town with my Grand-mama Juliana. She begs them to hide my father in their attic, if she can manage to smuggle him out of the Ghetto. She is making arrangements to have him cross the border into Romania so it would only be for a day or two. Ferenc refuses. In fact, his brother is later hanged as a Nazi collaborator.

Mother manages to smuggle Father out of the Ghetto. Before crossing the border—knowing he will be gone for a long stretch—he decides to come and see me, his beloved daughter, one last time. He is captured on the road to my hiding place.

He was transported to Auschwitz the next morning.

My mother is devastated. Before her conversion, she had been a church attending Catholic, and now she feels the need to seek her God. She walks into a church during a sermon. The priest is preaching to the congregation telling them, "You must root out the Jews among you, every man, woman, and child. It is your Christian duty." My mother stands up, approaches the pulpit, spits on the floor. She never enters a church again for the rest of her life.

The Russians start to attack anew here and I am able to leave the barn and go home to mother. All the Jews are gone and gleeful strangers move into their houses. It is strange not seeing Istvanka, or the old lady down the street walking her little dog. I feel very sad but soon the bombs start falling and sadness turns to a strange excitement. Children cannot conceive of their own mortality. I am not afraid of the noise. A bomb falls into the garden two houses away. It hits a gaming casino of some sort because there are rummy cubes and playing cards everywhere. It was snowing cards. Then a bomb falls in the back of our apartment building, which does not explode. It just makes a huge hole. There is no water, no electricity, and the only heat is in the kitchen from the wood heated cooking stove. When the sirens sound we all have to go to the basement. This happens so often, that my mother puts me to bed in a big wicker basket at night, and simply carries me down still asleep to the basement. My cat Lily has a kitten. During one of the bombardments, she is so frightened she eats it. I see it and cry for days.

There is a man in the building, an invalid, who can speak English and every day we all huddle around a field radio listening to London. News start trickling in about the concentration camps but mother does not believe it. After all, her Erno is a forty-five year old, strong, vital, healthy, and resourceful man. He will manage to come back to us.

We were getting very hungry.

I am watching the street from the window. A poor starved horse struggles to pull a cart piled high with furniture and household goods. The horse stumbles. The carter whips it to make it stand up, but the horse cannot move. It lies there with its eyes closed and doesn't breathe. I cry for the poor horse. I cry because my cat ate her kitten. I cry because I miss my father. He will come home soon and put everything right. Suddenly the street is teeming with women holding knives and bowls cutting into the still steaming carcass. In a few minutes there are only bones left, until most of the bones too are taken away to make soup.

Somebody finds potatoes in the basement. We eat potatoes for a long time. It is amazing how many ways you can cook a potato. It is getting very cold. It snows a lot.

After a time, we stop running to the basement when the sirens sound. The battle is very close. We can watch it from our window. The Russians cross the frozen river and start moving up the banks, linking arms and singing. They must be drunk. Nobody can be this brave. As they are advancing they are mowed down by machine guns from bunkers in the park in front of our house. They still keep coming. The mound of the dead growing into hills that they climb over. Still coming, and still singing, the mound getting higher and higher until the machine guns fall silent and we are under Russian occupation. We were all happy because finally the war is over.

We go into the woods to look for mushrooms to eat because we are very hungry. There are dead soldiers lying all around us. I am frozen in place and can't move forward for fear. Mother takes my hand and we jump over a dead man together. Slowly it becomes a game and the dead are simply an obstacle. My fear is gone.

Mother cheers for the Russians. They are going to get rid of the Nazis and their collaborators and allow the Jews to come home. So I cheer too. Maybe they are going to bring me some toys. Just in case they are not all friendly my mother and I hide in an airshaft. We wear all our clothes, wrap up in lots of blankets, and the snow covers us up so only our eyes are showing. It is very cold.

Grandma Juliana

There is a lot of screaming, and I later learn the Russian soldiers were raping women. Grandmama is living with us at this time but she is old and very fat so they leave her alone crying in the kitchen. When my mother finds out what happened she constructs a hiding place at one end of our bathroom. You have to go through the back of a wardrobe to get in there. She hangs some clothes in the cupboard and several women hide there. We find out our English speaker can also speak Russian. My mother dresses in some rags, puts a pillow on her back to look like a hunchback, smears soot on her face, blackens her teeth, and marches off with her interpreter to see the Russian commander. The commander is a woman! My mother immediately offers to make her dresses and, having no materials, she cuts up one of our curtains. When the commander comes for a fitting my mother has her take off her corset and a dreadful heavy-duty cone shaped bra that laces up on the back. When she tries on her dress, the commander looks pretty and feminine. This is what saves us from abuse and hunger.

The commander puts armed guards at our house and arranges for food to be delivered to us. We get everything—ham, butter, flour, a chicken, fruit, and even chocolate. The women from the hiding place, Grand-mama, my mother, and I feast royally by candlelight. The commander brings some more female soldiers to have dresses made. All our curtains and bedspreads are used up. The hidden women are put to work unpicking curtains and old clothes to provide cloth for new dresses. I am asleep on a cot in the kitchen when a drunk guards starts touching me. My grandmother hits him on the head with a rolling pin. Under normal circumstances she would be shot, but the commander makes arrangements. The soldier recovers and we are not punished.

A lot of the houses in our street are destroyed during the fighting. While walking past what used to be Istvanka's house, I find a piece of the plaster bust of him in the gutter. I pick up the piece. It is one of his curls and part of his forehead. I hold onto that piece of plaster for many years.

The town looks different. Some houses are burnt out, others collapsed. Although the trams still run, there is a silence around us. Most of the shops are closed or looted. The people walk around in shocked silence. I am very free—there is no school, no one to discipline me. I don't have to wash. I eat when hungry and roam around with some other children all over the ruins, playing until darkness falls. Mother works all the time to provide for us and has no time to look after me. I slowly realize that we are poor. Being poor means not having everything — no new toys and no new clothes. But above all, it is cold, so very cold.

Mother finds us a much better apartment on Main Street. I love the move. I am sitting on the end of a big flat cart piled with our furniture and household goods. I am dangling my feet, watching the flames that are spewing through the windows of the town hall. The flames are reflected in the puddles on the road. It is exciting to move to where the electricity is working and there aren't any unexploded bombs in the backyard. Our new home it is a beautiful place. The rooms are huge. They have very high ceilings with plaster moldings and dark red felt wall coverings. The floors are inlaid parquet with patterns made by different colored wood. We have Louis XVI furniture my parents are proud of and, for some reason, not one, but two grand pianos. The tall double doors have cut crystal panes. In each room there is an ornate, enclosed, round ceramic wood stove. The apartment takes up the whole floor and there is a grand curved staircase leading down to the vestibule, which opens into the courtyard. The courtyard has a huge wooden door that opens onto the street. Behind this house there are two apartments in another building with a garden in the middle. The concierge has a separate little apartment under our staircase. The gate is locked at ten o'clock at night and unless you have a key you have to ring for the concierge to wake up and let you in.

The Russian commander arranges for a young captain, Ivan, and his adjutant to come and live with us. Ivan is just eighteen, very young for a captain but so many have been killed and they are short of soldiers. Ivan is tall and blond and very beautiful. I love him with all my heart and spend a lot of time with him. He is very kind to me, always bringing me toys or something good to eat. His adjutant is an older stout man who has a lot of metal teeth. He plays the accordion and sings beautiful Russian songs—sometimes happy ones and sometimes sad ones, crying while he sings. They both drink all the time, anything with alcohol. They even drink perfume. I watch them bite off the neck of glass bottles, spit out the shards of glass with the blood and drink the contents. When they are very drunk they use the cherubs on the ceiling moldings for target practice. When we run out of wood for the stoves they chop up some of the antique furniture and burn it.

Jozsi, our interpreter, moves in with us too. I don't know why he is not in the army. It must be because of his disability. The Russians can't understand why they needed to liberate Hungary. After all, we live in such luxury compared to Russians! The Russians love watches and women, in that order. "Davai chas" and "Davai barishnia" (give me the watch and give me the woman) are the most heard commands. Compared to the dreadful things that were done to people in Russia, our occupiers are not too bad. They all love music and children.

One day Ivan brings us a raw goose liver. It is bloody so he decides to wash it in the toilet. When he pulls the chain the goose liver disappears. He becomes furious and shoots the toilet. Then we have another party and sing and I pretend to be a ballerina. I dance for my Ivan. I am happy. He calls me Katyushka.

I am ill with a fever. Ivan brings me an orange wrapped in white tissue paper. I don't remember ever having an orange. I un-wrap the beautiful round object and breathe in the exquisite fragrance. It looks like the rising sun. I hold it and just smell it for a whole day. The next day mother peels it and feeds me the delicious sweet segments. I am in heaven. The fragrant peels are boiled with sugar and kept in a jar. I am only allowed to eat it when I am ill. I want to be ill all the time.

When they are leaving, Ivan promises to come back for me in twelve years, when I am seventeen and marry me. I cried for days. My father is gone and now Ivan too.

I often wonder if he ever did come back for me or if he even survived the war? Some Russians are still in our town but move into army quarters. I lie in my bed listening to them marching in the street below, singing, always singing. The trains start bringing back some people who survived the camps.

"Hurry up and get ready," says Mother. *"Maybe your father will be on the train today!"*

We walk to the railway station and wait on the platform. The train comes in and we stand there. My mother holds a photo of Papa asking anyone who comes off the train if they had seen him. These people frighten me. They are like skeletons in rags. They have shaved heads. They shuffle slowly and smell.

She takes some of them home to our apartment where she washes them, delouses them and asks questions. After she burns their clothes she dresses them in Father's clothes, or her own if they are women. They all look alike to me I don't know how she can tell the difference. Some leave to go home to wherever home might be. A few stay longer, but nobody has any news of father. They start recounting their terrible experiences in the camps. I hide and listen.

Mother cries a lot, and I have nightmares every night, but I still, want to hear it. I want to know.

The photograph my mother showed people at the railway

Mother takes in a ten-year-old girl who came back from the camps. She tells me we are going to be like sisters. I can't remember her name. All I remember is being very uneasy around her. She makes me play sex games I don't like, and I don't dare tell anyone. A few months later a nineteen-year-old brother comes back from the camps, finds her, and takes her away. I am very relieved. It is only now that I wonder what horrible things were done to that child in the camps. How little compassion children have for each other. I still feel guilty for not liking her more, the poor little child. Poor little victim.

We visit the train station every day just to walk home sadly. Nobody knows what happened to father. I am sure he simply lost his memory. When he gets better and remembers me he will come home. I miss him so much.

A man shuffles over to us at the station. Mother doesn't recognize him but he knows her. He tells her he is the owner of "Pannonia," the big hotel next to the Opera. He remembers Mother and Father who played cards in the hotel's club every week. *"Don't wait for him Gabriella,"* he says. *"He is not coming back."* This poor broken man, who had nowhere else to go, eventually became my stepfather. Out of two broken families they cobbled together a whole one.

He was in the camp with Father and knows he died. He pulls out a tattered photo of me that Papa had hidden in his shoe when he died. Mother is devastated. I don't believe Father is dead. He would never leave me. I am sure he will come back!

Before he lost his mind to Alzheimer's my stepfather finally told me how my father died. We never told my mother. She never knew.

Photo found in
Father's shoe

My father and a friend from home stole some bread. They were caught, beaten half to death, and were made an example of. They were placed in dog cages in the middle of the open "parade ground" where every morning the inmates were counted. It was bitter cold; my father was left naked to die. It took two nights and a day. I often think of his death and cry. How could a strong, kind, young man in his prime be reduced to a naked broken shivering thing in a dog cage? What were his last thoughts? Did he question or deny his God? Was he delirious? Was death welcome?

Oh, Papa, I don't really know who you were. What kind of a man were you? Were you intelligent? Did you believe in God? Did you read a lot? Did you like music? I know you loved me. I wish you had lived. Lived with us and grown old with us. I wish, I wish, I wish...

My stepfather's name was also Erno. My father's name was Rubin, my stepfather's was Ruder. Same name, same initials. Before my mother could persuade him to come home with us he needed to go to Romania to see his mother. Mother gave him some money for the train. Still dressed in rags, after a long journey he arrived at his mother's house and knocked on the door. His mother opened the door and thought he was a beggar. She did not recognize him.

When my stepfather came back to Nagyvarad he went to see his family's faithful servant with whom they left everything for safekeeping. She opened the door wearing one of his wife's dresses. "Oh! I never expected any of you to survive. Well anyway the Russians took everything!" she said, slamming the door in his face.

He moved in with us and slowly my mother nursed him back to health. Erno, who went by the musical nickname of "Piccolo," was the son of a minor functionary in a small Romanian town called Petroseni. As I remember, I am constantly amazed how well educated he was, coming

Ernest Ruder and sister as children

from not much money, and just a regular high school. Of course he spoke German, Hungarian (his mother tongue), Romanian, and French. He also had a very good knowledge of Latin and some Greek. He knew Roman history and Greek mythology inside out and frequently quoted Latin to me. He played the piano and composed music. Yet he never learned to read music. I suppose it was all talent. He had been a very

Ernst Ruder in
amateur Theatricals

cultured musician who married the only daughter of a wealthy Jewish family. They moved to Nagyvarad and bought the Pannonia—hotel, club, and restaurant on the square where the Opera stood. With his father-in-law they ran the business. His wife Manci stayed home to look after their little girl Ditta.

They were all deported together—mother-in-law, father-in-law, Manci, aged 31, and Ditta, aged 11. My stepfather was sent to the right side to work. The rest were sent to the left and were gassed that same day . When he asked an inmate who had been there longer where they took the families, the man pointed to a tall chimney, belching smoke. *"There they are,"* he said.

The Pannonia Hotel, where my parents played rummy every Saturday night

One of the guards found out that Piccolo played the violin. For fun the guard broke the fingers on his right hand. The bones were never set and his hand remained damaged. He could still play the piano but not the violin.

Of the many terrible stories about the camps, one sticks in my mind most. When the Americans liberated my stepfather's camp during the last phase of the war, he was barely alive. By this time only survival mattered. There were no tears left. He lay dying when a soldier addressed him in halting Yiddish. *"How are you feeling?"* he said to the poor emaciated man. Erno saw his chance and whispered to the soldier: *"Do you know who I am?"* The soldier said he didn't. *"But I am Ernest Ruder!"* The soldier felt he might be important and he got special treatment, which saved his life.

Erno Ruder was a broken man. He and my mother slowly

Ernest Ruder, wife Manci, aged 31, and daughter Ditta, aged 11

drifted into marriage. It was never great love or passion, but more of a logical arrangement, especially since he was very good to me. I somehow replaced his dead child. When he was dying—in the final stages of Alzheimer's—in his poor confused mind she and I became one, and he would call me Ditta. I have often wondered how anyone who survived the camps, who lost children and family, could go on living. As a child I remember visiting friends of my parents both in Nagyvarad and later Israel. So many of them had photographs of dead children. Those people went on to live and laugh, work and live, have other new children, but it seems that towards the end of their lives the past takes over. Many survivors commit suicide and others take refuge in madness where reality and horror no longer exist.

As a child, my favorite story was "The Blue Bird" by Maeterlinck. Two children, a brother and sister go wandering in the woods following a blue bird and come to a house in a clearing. The door opens and their grandparents welcome them smiling. "But you are both dead!" say the children. "How come you are here?" "Well" says the grandfather, "When you remember us and think about us with love, we are indeed alive."

Sometimes, in the silence of the night when all is still, I think of little Ditta, aged 11. I wish I could bring her back with love, and let her live a long life like the one given to me by sheer luck. Ditta had been a happy child. She loved to play the piano. She went to dancing school, loved to read, and laughed a lot. I have often imagined her dying in the gas chamber, fighting for a last breath. I want to feel her agony in order to alleviate the guilt I feel for being alive. After I die there will be nobody left to remember Ditta.

Ditta, age 11,
when she was gassed

One of the great tragedies of the Holocaust, other than the killing and torture and horror, is all the potential that has been extinguished. How many writers, artists, musicians, philosophers, scientists, and geniuses were among the victims or their unborn children? What would have become of Istvanka had he lived? Ditta? All my cousins? All the Jewish children of Nagyvarad?

I have battled survivor guilt all my life. If I had not been hidden, my father wouldn't have been caught. Why was I spared when so many other children who were more clever and kinder that me died? Why was I singled out to live?

I became an overachiever. I have to make my life count somehow. I have to try and make a difference. I cannot retire. I don't have time to die. I need to keep on. I owe it to the others who were never given a chance to live.

Around the age of seven I got angry and denied God.

Papa had been a good and kind man. He never hurt anyone and always gave money to the poor, and yet God let them kill him and the rest of the family. If God is this nasty I don't want to know him. He is not a nice God. I don't want anything to do with him. I have never been able to believe again.

We still live in Nagyvarad, but under the communists. Now my family is persecuted, not for being Jewish, but because they are middle-class. "Bourgeois" becomes the new epithet that allows the bullies of society to pick on others. The people who worshipped authority and toed the line under the Nazis now became good communists, denouncing, persecuting, and bullying others. My mother is forced to take back the woman who denounced her to the Nazis because she needs a job and the authorities need a spy in her business.

Kati, first communion

Under pressure from Grand-mama I have first communion. I am dressed like a bride, and because it was cold, I have a short white fur jacket. My photograph is displayed in a local photographer's window for years, all retouched like some movie starlet. I feel very important.

Mother decides to enroll me in the Catholic school run by nuns. It smells of floor polish and incense. The nuns are either kind or really nasty.

We have to start each page with a row of flowers on the top line. My flowers are sloppy so I am made to kneel on dry corn in the corner. It really hurts.

The next day my flowers are still sloppy so I have to hold my hand up with the fingertips bunched. The nun hits my fingers with a ruler. I cry for a long time.

One day the oldest nun dies and is laid in state in the chapel. We all have to file past the open coffin, sprinkle holy water on the dead nun, and kiss her on the forehead. Her skin is the coldest thing I ever felt. I saw corpses during the war, but she is the one I have nightmares about for years.

Before Easter vacation we have an assembly where the mother superior warns us about being caught by Jews who will use our innocent blood to make Passover bread. I go home and tell my mother. "That's it!" she says and marches me off to the convent. The mother superior is in her office and doesn't want to see us. Mother kicks the door open, calls her an old whore, and spits on her desk. This was the end of my Catholic education.

Mother makes dresses for a singer at the Opera, who gives me some old crowns that are no longer needed. I am in heaven! To appear on stage I need a theatre, so I enlist all the kids who live next door in a big apartment building and we put on plays in our hallway. The curtain is a sheet on a wire, but the costumes (thanks to my mother) are great! I write the plays in a way that I always end up with the starring role and wear the crown. We charge admission and every actor has to sell at least two tickets. We have good ticket sales, and reinvest the money in the next play. This goes on for about two years. It was during this time that my love for theatre became a lifelong passion.

I am enrolled in the regular school where lessons are in Romanian. I have no trouble learning the language and also pick up Russian, which is being taught as a second language.

Grand-mama, my maternal grandmother, Aunt Aranka, her husband Ferenc, and their baby move in with us. According to the authorities we have too many rooms. After the war, as many buildings were damaged, some of us have to go to school in the afternoon. Grand-mama takes me to ballet and has ambitions to make me into a dancer. Ballet is in the afternoon and so is school. Unbeknown to my mother, grand--mama prefers ballet so I don't go to school for months. Eventually the inspector comes and I am sent back to school. I have to stand up in front of the whole school, tell them what I did wrong, and do what is called "self-criticism." I am terribly ashamed.

Grand-mama is no longer allowed to go out with me except on Sundays. So Sunday morning we go to church and Sunday afternoon we take the tram to the last station where grand-mama does some serious drinking in a sleazy workingmen's bar. It has a long zinc counter and she can catch drinks the bartender slides to her without losing a drop. She sings all the way home.

She makes an altar in the room we share and makes me pray every night for my mother's soul because she is doomed for marrying not one, but two Jews. Soon after this, my stepfather's mother and his two nieces move in with us too. The older of the girls and my stepfather play the two grand pianos in tandem. It sounds very beautiful. Mother sends me for piano lessons. A few weeks later the teacher comes and tells my mother she would rather "pay" not to have to teach me. That is the end of my musical career.

I manage to get some silk worms and find that housing them in one of the grand pianos is a logical idea. You have no idea what a colony of silk worms can do to a piano.

My Jewish step-grandmother starts taking me to Synagogue every Saturday and a monumental battle ensues for my soul. Frankly, I prefer church. It is colorful and gaudy and smells of incense. Synagogue is bare and we have to sit upstairs, away from the action. The result of this battle is that I am still totally disinterested in religion of any kind.

Mother, Step-grandma Ruder, and Stepfather

The Romanian children pick on me because I speak Hungarian. The Hungarians pick on me because I speak good Romanian. They hate me because I learn Russian quickly. They all pick on me because I am a "stinking Jew." One day, walking home from school, some boys catch me and cut off one of my long braids. I run home sobbing, carrying my shorn braid. I also become very angry. "I'll show them!" I think.

Because of my linguistic talents I become the best student in my class. I am awarded the distinction of being a "pioneer." I receive a red silk scarf which only one student gets in each class. We pioneers are also indoctrinated in communist concepts and get to march up and down Main Street on important Communist national days. I am given a big heavy drum. I carry it with great pride while my family stands on our balcony of our house and cheers.

On my way to school I have to cut through a park next to a building that is only referred to in whispers by grownups. It is the "Securitate" building. People who disappear are taken there. I often hear bloodcurdling screams coming from the blacked out windows. At schools we are told only enemies of the state are punished. They are all criminals and bloodsuckers.

My classroom has large portraits of Lenin, Stalin, Marx, and Engels on the wall. We are taught that Stalin is the greatest leader on earth and we are so very lucky to live under Communism. Of course, not everyone is as enlightened as us. To help our parents we are to report any anti-communist conversations in our homes so the authorities can help retrain them politically. I duly report my mother. She is punished by having to do volunteer labor every Sunday for a year. She has to plant heavy benches in public places. They stop discussing politics in front of me.

At this point, I make a beautiful emblem of communist Romania in a collage of colored rice and write a poem in Romanian and Russian entitled "War or Peace?" I send all this to Stalin; I am still waiting for a thank you.

My conversion against communism happens when they confiscate our apartment and all our furniture. We are given one large room in which we all have to live—mother, my stepfather, the two grandmothers, my stepfather's two nieces, myself, and the maid. That night I manage to sneak into what had been our living room and unscrew an ornament from the Louis XVI table. I hide the ornament and start hating the communists. There are two kitchens in the apartment, so we have our own kitchen at least. We have to share the bathroom with strangers. This doesn't

Some of our confiscated furniture Stepfather's niece on right

upset me because I am not too fond of washing at this point. Bathing once a week is just fine with me.

We still have a maid, which is acceptable. Her name is Piri and she is a very happy peasant girl. One day I find her in the kitchen trying to weigh her breasts to see if they both weigh the same. She cooks our meals. Food is very scarce at this point and a lot of my mother's customers pay in eggs, meat, or butter. Mother wants to train me to run a home so I have to go with Piri to the market once a week and help buy and plan meals. Piri can't read, write, or count, so I am in charge of finances. It makes me feel very important.

We have four ducks that are being fattened for Christmas. We have cherries preserved in rum that spoiled in the pantry, so Grand-mama throws the lot out into the snow. The ducks eat it. The ducks are found outside lifeless and Piri and Grand-mama quickly pluck them and leave them by the stove in the kitchen to gut and cook later in the day. The ducks wake up from their drunken stupor and find they are completely naked. They can't be let out because of the cold. My mother, ever resourceful, finds a piece of black and white checked woolen material and makes them little coats with sleeves! They look wonderful parading and quacking around the yard in their little coats.

Once a year we buy a pig. I hate it because it is slaughtered in the yard. I can hear it screaming in terror and pain. I hide and cover my ears. Every part of the pig is used. The guts are washed and used for sausages. The fresh blood is mixed with spices and rice and used as "blood sausage." The bacon and hams are smoked in a special room next to the pantry. The liver is used in liver sausage. The cheeks and tongue are made into a special sausage with gelatin that comes from boiling the trotters. There was something called *"Kocsonya"* which is pieces of meat in aspic also made from the trotters. The only parts thrown away are the teeth and the anus. Even the tail is roasted and eaten. The fat is rendered down and used in cooking and the bones are boiled for soup. Nothing is ever wasted. By the time the smoking is done I forget how the poor pig died and eat heartily. Thankfully, my Jewish step-grandmother doesn't keep kosher and has no problem eating pork, although her best dish remains the *"Cholent."* She cooks it with beans and a stuffed gooseneck. Her job is fattening the lone goose we always keep. She holds it down and stuffs food down its gullet every day. The goose liver still lives in my memory as the best food I ever ate. It is strange that things I now feel are disgusting and inhuman were so acceptable. That is how it always was. Who was I to question it? Anyway children were not asked their opinions.

My stepfather's sister Stefania marries a Jewish pharmacist who had been widowed in Romania. They move to a long peasant house on the main road in a village in the Transylvanian mountains where uncle Hendrik opens a pharmacy. I am sent there every vacation. The house has no electricity and the toilet is an outhouse. It consists of a hole cut in a wooden plank, which covers a deep pit. We have to draw water from a well and wash in a tin bath in the kitchen. There is a big garden behind the house with a stream across the back. I have wonderful times playing in the mud with tadpoles and frogs. I have no friends and have to resort to amusing myself. I climb trees, roam in the fields, and climb into the attic above the house where I can look down on the road through chinks in the tiles. Once a week it is market day and the peasants come into the village all dressed in their finery.

Being an only child makes you more resourceful because you spend a lot of time observing human nature rather that just playing with siblings. I start leaving little boxes in the road and watch. People look around to see no one is looking and pocket the box. I realize they are greedy and I want to teach them a lesson. I go to a neighbor's cowshed, get some manure, put it into little boxes and leave them on the road. The greedy peasants pocket the boxes and I can only imagine how they react when the box starts oozing in the warmth of their pockets.

There are a lot of flies, so uncle Hendrik pays me a certain sum of money per hundred flies I have killed. I have to line up the dead flies in groups of ten by ten so he can count them. I soon realize I can double my income by cutting each fly into two with a razor blade and carefully line them up on the newspaper in the usual groups mixing them up a bit so the sizes are different. He never finds out. Or perhaps the dear man never tells me?

The house next to ours in Nagyvarad is a large block of apartments with several children living in them. I make friends with a lot of them, including a simpering mama's boy called Ede, who we take up to the attic to play doctors. One of the experiments is pulling on the poor boy's penis, and measuring with a ruler, to see how many centimeters he could go before crying. I am not proud of this. Somewhere there must be a man called Ede with serious sexual issues.

After the war, children are much freer to roam around with friends. We no longer have nannies and governesses and our parents were all busy trying to put food on the table.

There is a tall building in the center of town—the suicides' regular place to jump. I am roaming around with a bunch of neighborhood kids when we hear that someone had just jumped off the eighth floor onto the cobblestones in the courtyard. We all run as fast as we can and get there as the police drive in. Before they can stop us we all have a good look at the poor man whose head split open like a melon spilling his brains all over the cobblestones. I have seen dead people before but never exposed brains. It is pinkish white not unlike the scrambled egg with calf's brains we eat at home. I never eat brains after that.

I had never seen a black man until one arrives in town. He must have come with the Russians. We all run to look at him. He is a tall, kindly man who tolerates our ignorance and curious stares. Being braver that the others, I lick my index finger and start rubbing his wrist to see if the color will come off. He laughs and shows me his pink palms. I am totally confused and he laughs heartily. *Simone, dear granddaughter, little did I know you would come into my life and my heart, and looking into your beautiful eyes I would imagine Africa.*

Things are getting worse for us. We are not working-class enough and so my parents tell me we are going to try and immigrate to a country called Israel. Everybody in Israel is Jewish and so we won't be persecuted, and it is all right to be middle-class. We have to get photographs taken for the exit permits. We are supposed to look unsavory and brutish so the communists want to get rid of us. My stepfather has not shaved for several days and I am instructed to look stupid. Judging from the photo I do a great job.

My parents tell me that Israel is full of oranges and lovely white villas perched on the mountain side, that the sun always shines and life will be fun and easy. After a few months we get our permit and are told we can only take a suitcase full of personal clothes—no jewelry and no gold watches. We are only permitted to bring plain metal watches. Suddenly people are bartering gold watches for plain metal ones.

Mother, myself and my stepfather looking brutish for passport photo

It is night. We are behind Uncle Hendrick's house digging a hole under one of the windows. The moon is very bright. Mother shows me jewels in a shoebox. There are pearls, rubies, a diamond necklace, emeralds, and lots of gold rings, bracelets, and brooches. The one I remember most is a brooch of an exotic looking lady in ivory with a jeweled crown and necklace. The shoebox is almost full. They wrap the box in a towel and bury it deep in the soil. Mother tells me this is my inheritance.

Our day of departure arrives. Everybody cries a lot. We all know we will never see each other again. We go to the train station in a horse drawn taxi. Grand-mama waves goodbye, crying.

We packed suitcases with clothes and precious photographs. All that is left of our world. We are allowed to take some food for the journey.

As we go through the customs. The woman checking me notices a thin chain with a little medallion around my neck. My father had given it to me. It is the only thing I have left from him. Not bothering to open the clasp, she rips is off my neck cutting me slightly. I am eleven years old and very upset. She laughs and pockets my chain.

We go by train to Constanza where we board a ship called "TRANSYLVANIA." It was built for six hundred passengers. There are over a thousand people and at least as many roaches and rats on board. Still, there is palpable excitement and relief in the air. Everyone is happy to leave Romania. We make the best of it. My parents take turns sleeping so the one on duty can keep the roaches and rats off me and the other person sleeping.

There is a man on board who was a communist commissar and caused many people to get arrested. They probably allowed him to go to Israel to spy. The men wrap him in a blanket and beat him severely. He remains in the infirmary during the journey. The beating cures him of communism.

People often ask me if I ever go back to visit my birthplace? No! Why would I want to go back to where so much blood was shed, where they hunted me, captured my father, and sent him to his death—where they tortured my mother, rounded up men, women, and children, and helped murder them only because they were Jewish? Why would I walk the streets where we were all so happy and then so unhappy? Why would I want to revisit the charnel house that Nagyvarad has become for me? I recall my childhood with fondness, the childhood given to me by my parents, not by Nagyvarad. It would be too painful to reopen the wounds.

What if the holocaust had never happened? What if, what if?

My aunt Bozsi died this morning. Her nurse called me to say she passed away peacefully in her sleep. "A very good death," she said. Bozsi was my mother's youngest sister. She the last thread connecting me to a world that no longer exists—Nagyvarad, of my happy early childhood and the place where so much was lost—a place I never want to see again.

My mother was eleven years older than my aunt and when Bozsi turned fifteen she came to live with my parents. My mother wanted her to get an education. Bozsi had other ideas. She was a pretty girl with an irresistible smile and soon started sneaking out to hang out with boys. She and a girlfriend went around cafes, smoking cigarettes, becoming promiscuous, and getting into bad company. Nagyvarad was a small town. Bozsi's behavior soon came to my mother's attention and she forbade her sister to go out without a chaperone. A tutor came daily to educate her, but she was rebelling against my mother's control.

She ran away with an older boy and got on a slow train to a nearby town. I don't know how, but my mother found out where they were heading, took a carriage, and waited for them at their destination. When they got off the train mother beat up the boy and after slapping her sister around took Bozsi back with her. Having realized that normal education was not for Bozsi, she tried to find some other career for her. Bozsi asked to learn to dance so she was enrolled in the best dance studio money could buy.

She ran away again and joined a dance troupe called "Ballet de Violettas" run by a man called Mr. Sebok and his wife. This troupe traveled around the Mediterranean eventually making their base in North Africa. The six girls danced the can-can and other burlesque numbers and after the performance they drank with the patrons. Sex with the patrons, though not obligatory, was encouraged. They always stayed in good hotels, had nice clothes but most of the money was pocketed by Mr. Sebok. The girls got only pocket money. He was "looking after their money" for them. The girls were all Hungarian or Romanian and after the war broke out none of them wanted to go home, even if they could. Mr. Sebok and his wife had a strangle hold on these girls. Bozsi always spoke of them with great affection. She loved the nightlife and the excitement and did not communicate much with her family at home.

Bozsi had a beautiful figure an amazing smile and a happy disposition. When she was performing in Tangier a young English diplomat fell in love with her. He bought her out of the troupe, set up house with her, and made plans to marry her. He was from some upper-class noble family. When his mother found out about his plans, she flew out to Tangier and had her son committed to a mental institution. Some priests ran the dubious mental home, and when Bozsi tried to visit him there she was threatened and called a whore. She was broken-hearted and went back to Mr. Sebok. There was nothing else she could do. The English boy remained the love of her life.

One of the girls disappeared and was found murdered on the beach. She had been Bozsi's best friend. No one was ever arrested for her murder although she was last seen in the company of an important man .The girl was twenty-three.

Bozsi met a very distinguished French diplomat named Henri. He fell deeply in love with her. Henri had a wife and family in France but loved Bozsi until he died.

After the war, Bozsi met a Jewish concert pianist who escaped the Holocaust. He was earning a living playing the piano in the best hotel in Tangier. He was a mild mannered, sweet man. After they got married Bozsi stayed home. She didn't have to work. During this period, she reconnected with her family at home, and although by no means wealthy, she was extremely generous and giving. Just after the war when we had very little to eat, she would send us packages with coffee, chocolate, and sardines, a great delicacy! Mother got some butter and mixed it with the sardines in to stretch it. I still remember the taste of the sardines and butter on thick black bread. One day she sent me a nylon raincoat. I remember the smell of it as I unpacked it and tried it on.

No one in Nagyvarad had anything as glamorous as that. She also sent me a transparent red nylon comb, which became my prized possession. There was cocoa in one of the parcels and big tablets of Swiss chocolate. It was like Christmas.

I first met Bozsi when she came to visit us in Israel when I was twelve. I still remember her radiant smile. I bonded with her immediately, and she was my favorite relative. Later as I became a teen, whenever my parents disapproved of my behavior they would say I had inherited "Bozsi's bad blood." I didn't care. I liked her.

Bozsi remained faithful to her husband and bore him a daughter, Kinga. When Kinga was six or seven, Bozsi's husband died of a heart attack and she decided to move to America where she had a brother-in-law and my parents who had moved there too. She went to work in the fur industry as a seamstress and raised her child.

When Henri found out about Bozsi's circumstances, he started sending her money and flew her many times to Paris. He helped with Kinga's education and loved Bozsi very much, but because he had a retarded daughter, he could not leave his wife. Years later, Bozsi received a phone call from his wife. Henri was on his deathbed and asked to speak to Bozsi. His wife handed the phone to him and he said a tearful good-bye to his love.

Bozsi and her daughter were not very close, but Bozsi and my mother became closer in their old age and spent time together mainly in New York. After my mother died I moved Bozsi to New Hampshire and became her support until this morning.

My Aunt Bozsi (furthest to the right)

II.
ISRAEL

We sail into Haifa bay at dawn. Everyone is on deck watching the sunrise over Mount Carmel. Dawn starts red and then turns to gold. There are white villas perched on the hills and it is warm, just like we were told. An old man in his prayer shawl is sobbing and praying on deck. As we disembark he falls to his knees and kisses the ground.

We are herded into a large hall and asked to line up. We are doused with DDT powder. We mill around waiting to find out what comes next. There are buses taking people to refugee camps.

My parents make a different decision. Instead of joining the others and going to a refugee camp with tents, my parents decide to stay in Haifa. We get on a bus to Mount Carmel and check into an elegant hotel.

My parents sit me in the lobby and tell me to find customers for my mother. It never occurs to me to feel shy or scared. I was brought up to feel I could do anything, so I sit in the lobby and wait. I can speak four languages, so when I hear one of the languages spoken I go up to the ladies and tell them about my mother's talents. Although I was only eleven, I must have been very convincing. Mother soon had enough customers to pay for the hotel and for whatever food was available at the time in Israel. The food consisted mainly of eggplants and a type of yogurt called "Lebenia". There was other food but those were at very high prices. We ate the three Hungarian salamis we brought with us.

Stepfather and I,
Tel Aviv

Eventually I had to go to school, so my parents reluctantly found a boarding school for me. I started having bad vibes as soon as we drove onto the campus. The office was in the school building but the dorms were long huts, away from the main building. If ever there was a misnomer "Mosad Ahava" was it. "Institute of Love," what a joke! It was the most miserable place for me. I couldn't speak a word of Hebrew and soon I became the butt of every joke. I was constantly bullied. I was regularly locked in the toilet, had water spilled on my bed, and was laughed at being the only outsider. The boys shot bits of sharpened wires into my legs with rubber bands and the girls pulled my hair daily. My parents came to visit and brought me a piece of chocolate which I tried to make last. It was taken from me the next day. I cried a lot and started to learn Hebrew. Necessity, rage, and thirst for revenge is the best teacher.

My mother found an old customer of hers who set her up in business in Tel-Aviv, so we finally left Haifa. At last! Housing was very scarce so my parents rented a room from an old German Jewish woman. Because she hated children I was only allowed to stay there one night a week. Back to boarding school again!

Miss J. B. Rosie

The nearest boarding school that would take me was "Tabeetha School" run by Church of Scotland missionaries. Miss J. B. Rosie, the headmistress, was one of the best and strongest influences in my life. She was a thin white-haired spinster with her hair in a bun under a snood. She spoke with a clipped upper-class Scottish accent, wore metal-rimmed glasses, and never had to raise her voice. Her mere presence was so powerful that all she had to do was stand in front of a hundred and fifty noisy children and within seconds you could hear a pin drop.

The school was in a beautiful old Arab house in Jaffa. The house had a huge garden, which was used as the playground. Miss Rosie had a small apartment at the back of the second floor and the "Hostel" as they called the boarding school was a short distance away. There was a big central hall in the school where every morning we had assembly. Miss Rosie's office was large and rather forbidding. She collected stuffed birds that were all lined up on top of the bookcases surrounding the room. The first time I was taken there I thought she would feed me to those scary birds.

In the "Hostel," which housed some thirty girls, we had two large dormitories, a shared shower room, and a separate toilet. Learning from my previous boarding school experience I knew that, being the new girl, I had to have a mentor. I befriended Haya who could speak German. The fact that she was the school bully actually helped a lot. I was not persecuted at all. I was protected and accepted by the other girls and actually enjoyed being there, except for the very large cockroaches that made frequent appearances, especially in the bathroom.

I quickly mastered English and after six months I took every academic prize. On what they called "speech day" we all wore white dresses. The boys wore white shirts and black trousers. We were called up onto a podium to receive congratulations and usually a book about bird watching—British bird watching. I never liked birds, not then, not now.

As much as I excelled at languages and academics, math was a struggle and sports were a real problem. I was a sickly child. We were playing volleyball when the ball hit my hand and fractured my arm. Miss Rosie personally walked me across the street to the French Hospital. I sat in the waiting room crying and asked her,

"Will it hurt?" "Yes, dreadfully," she replied. She believed in putting up with things and, above all, telling the truth.

My parents finally managed to rent an apartment I could also live in, so I left boarding school and traveled by bus daily to Jaffa. "Tabeetha" was the only English school in the area at the time. All the children of diplomats, foreign advisers, and contractors went to school there. They all seemed immensely rich to me. They had a lot of food. I saw an American boy throw away a banana after only one bite and was shocked. They wore different clothes every day, even different shoes. I had clothes because my mother made them for me, but shoes were another matter. One day I decided to paint my shoes to match my dress but it rained heavily that day. While lining up outside to enter the main hall I started leaving colored puddles as I walked. The rich kids laughed at me and I was terribly ashamed.

I loved school—the smell of wax, the ornate tiled floors, the echoing high ceiling rooms, cool in the summer heat, the sound of the bell—but above all, the calm and orderly hours and the books. I devoured books.

I think we all have done things that we regret and are ashamed of. One of the worst things I did was to falsely accuse a girl. Agneta lived with her parents in a ruined house near the school. They had a sort of room there with a sheet instead of a door, and no indoor plumbing. They were new emigrants also from Romania. Agneta was a shy, clever, gawky girl and not much liked by anyone. Some money was stolen from a girl in our class and seeing Agneta with an unusually large sum that day I went and told Miss Rosie. Poor Agneta was shamed. As it turned out, it was money her father had given her. She did not steal it. I did apologize at the time but now I feel so very sorry for harassing someone as poor and innocent as her. I will feel this shame and regret until I die.

My parents finally could afford to rent a nicer apartment but as the dressmaking business was housed there I didn't have my own room and had to sleep on a pullout bed in the room where mother's clients had their fittings.

When I was thirteen, two Danish brothers came to our school. Ole was the older, sixteen, and he was absolutely gorgeous. He was tall, blond, and very confident. Ole was my first serious love. I was a child, flat chested, and not exactly noticeable. He didn't even look at me. So I started asking him to help me with my math at recess and a friendship developed. There was a lovely sixteen-year-old buxom American girl after him also, and, when everyone went horseback riding I went along too. Never having sat on a horse, it took off with me through some trees. A branch slapped me across the face and I fell off, my face bleeding and hurting, though less than my wounded pride. The worst was seeing Ole and the buxom Bonnie riding off into the sunset oblivious to it all.

After a while Ole started looking at me and invited me to the movies. As I was getting ready, my mother was dressing too. "Where are you going?" I asked her. "With you, of course," she answered. She thought chaperoning me was the right thing to do. It took some effort to dissuade her. The cinema was around the corner, it was a matinee, and I would have died of embarrassment.

Ole, I, aged 13, and Ole's brother

This great love of mine was totally innocent. Just to be in his presence was enough. The weekends seemed never ending torture. All I could do was think of him. My grades started dropping until Miss Rosie called me into her office, wanting to know what the reason was. "I am in love," I told her. After all, she never told me a lie either. She was not very happy and told me schoolwork was more important than love. I did manage to get my grades up, especially as Ole's father was going back to Copenhagen. I cried a lot when they left and we corresponded until our engagement when I was seventeen.

I identified with my American friends and desperately wanted to be one of them. When riding the bus to school with American friends who lived nearby, I would pretend to be one of them. I was very much part of their circle and was invited to all their parties.

By now I was almost sixteen. Miss Rosie told me I could possibly get a full scholarship to Edinburgh University to study English literature. I was thrilled. My parents had different plans. "You will become a dressmaker and work in the family business," they declared. "You need a profession. Literature is not a profession." I didn't dream of contradicting them. You simply did what your parents told you. It was not a matter of choice. I left school with a heavy heart and started learning in my mother's sewing room supervised by her fifteen "girls." I hated every moment and to this day I do not touch a sewing needle unless I have to. I know how to do it but I don't tell anyone. If you can't sew, nobody can ask you to.

We are at the cinema with my parents. Before the film they show a recently found Nazi documentary showing twins who were used for medical

experiments. A terrible scream rends the silence. They stop the film. The lights go up and a woman is led out screaming, *"Those two little boys were mine and they are dead!"*

My parents were friends with a couple whose son Tomi was a budding journalist at the Hungarian Israeli daily called "Uj Kelet." He was twenty-four and though I was eight years younger than him I was allowed to go to the cinema with him because our parents knew each other. He gave me my first French kiss in front of a closed shop front at the central bus station. I was shocked but intrigued. Tomi was very upset that my parents educated me in a foreign school and robbed me of the possibility of assimilating into the fabric of Israel. He was right, but my parents thought they were doing what was best.

With Tomi

My stepfather and I are going to a soccer match. He is always so proud of me. We get off the bus and suddenly a man walking opposite stops in front of my stepfather. They stare at each other and then embrace, sobbing. They were bunkmates in the camp and each thought the other one was dead.

Once again, Miss. Rosie came to influence my life. She never wanted my mother to make her a dress, but she appeared one day with a piece of material and asked my mother to design a garment for her. During her last fitting mother accidentally stuck a pin through her waist. Not surprisingly, Miss. Rosie stood ramrod straight, smiling through the ordeal until the end of the fitting. When my mother tried to pull the dress off her, she was mortified at the torture she had inflicted on the poor woman. *"I'll do anything to put this right,"* Mother said. So Miss Rosie asked to have me come to her office two afternoons a week to further my education, and she would not take a penny for it!

She took my education in hand. She taught me history, geography, literature, art history, theatre, history of music, and ethics. She made me read more books and taught me to respect intellect. She gave me a love of language and literature for which I will be eternally grateful. She taught me for two years until I was taken to Paris. I still wonder what direction my life would have taken if I had been allowed to study in Edinburgh. What if? These crossroads happened several times in my life and I can't help feeling that there must be such a thing as fate. After all, life is totally unpredictable and so influenced by mere chance and serendipity. Missing a bus or meeting someone you haven't seen for a while can change the course of your life.

I was still corresponding with Ole Jepsen, my first love, but it did not stop me from enjoying my newfound popularity—going to many parties and outings with the American kids I had met in school. I had a very hectic social life and did not really miss out on being a teenager. Their lives seemed so easy compared to the rest of Israel.

I started modeling and earned quite a bit of money, which I spent, as you guessed, on shoes!

At this point, my parents decided that I had to further my education in Paris. Mother made me lots of cocktail and evening dresses—perhaps her idea of the life I was predestined to live. My

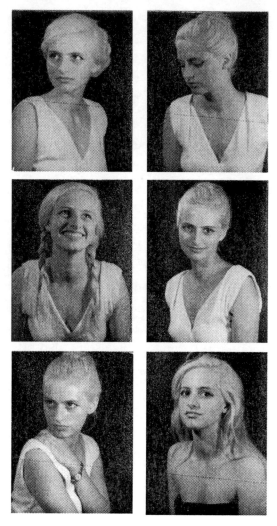

I, the teenager

stepfather and I sailed to Italy and then Marseilles. We took the train to Paris from there. How different this trip was from the last one with the rats and roaches! We had a lovely cabin and we got to sit at the captain's table (I don't know why). The food was great. I was almost seventeen and very pretty. When we entered a room all the men looked at me. I was drunk with my new power. The trip was great, being entertained and never sitting during dances. I felt very sophisticated and elegant, wearing a different glamorous dress every night. Travel in those days was leisurely and exclusive—no crowds, no delays, no security checks.

When the ship docked in Genoa, Italy, we went to visit its famous cemetery. It is an incredible place full of art. Each grave has a monument either depicting the dead person or some allegorical representation of death snatching a young girl or child. One grave has a statue of an old woman in simple clothes selling bagels.

Apparently the bagel seller saved up all her money during her lifetime in order to be buried in great style.

This was also the first time I met Germans since the war. I was shocked hearing German again, a language I refused to speak after they took my father. I peered into the faces of these middle-aged men, subconsciously searching for signs of a killer. I used to think you could tell if someone was capable of atrocities just by looking at their expression. It is only after I read *The Banality of Evil* by Hannah Arendt that I came to understand that people are capable of killing small children during the day only to later go home to dinner with their own children at night without remorse. It took me a long time to be able to set foot in Germany. It is easier now, a generation later, because the possible perpetrators are dead and I never believed in visiting the sins of the fathers upon their children.

Cover of *"Laisha"* Women's
Magazine, 1953

III.
PARIS

Our train arrived in Paris in the evening. It was raining and the city was grey. There was a woman on the train with us who was Hungarian and had spent her youth in Paris. I could not understand her tears of joy and her excitement at just being there. After I spent two years there, I too fell in love with the city, the language, the culture, and the food. I couldn't imagine living anywhere else in the world.

My stepfather found a Jewish youth hostel for me in Neuilly-Sur-Seine, a very elegant suburb, full of huge houses and quite a long walk from the Metro station's last stop.

He took me to the Follies Bergere, a sort of extravagantly elaborate revue theater where beautiful semi-nude men and women—mostly women— performed themed musical pieces. We met the director, a middle-aged Hungarian man who agreed to use one of my stepfather's compositions for one of the tableaus. It had something to do with Venice, with water, gondolas, and lots of breasts. It was performed a year later and of course it became the highlight of my stepfather's existence. Tears were running down his face during the performance when he came back to Paris to see it. The fact that the establishment was a huge draw for male tourists, especially South American cattle barons and Texan oilmen did not diminish his pride.

With Stepfather
in Paris

When Father departed after delivering me to Paris, he told me that I must go to work for Christian Dior who was, at the time, the most famous fashion designer in the world. My parents believed I could do anything. Even the impossible was just something I would find a way to solve. My parents' total belief in my ability gave me a lifelong supreme sense of self-confidence. To this day I believe I can tackle anything. Failure is just something that happens on the way to success. After all, if you don't fail sometimes, it means you haven't tried. I am now in my seventies and I still think I can fly. This is probably the greatest gift from my parents.

On the first day on my own, I went to a small restaurant and ordered the cheapest thing on the menu. My French was very poor. They

Photograph of the show at *Folies Bergeres* that featured one of my stepfather's musical compositions

brought me a boiled calf's head. The hairs were still on its snout! *"Tete de Veau Vinaigrette"* it was called. Ugh! It gave me incentive to learn French very quickly!

The youth hostel consisted of two large old houses, one for boys and one for girls. We got breakfast but had to fend for ourselves for the rest of our meals. There was a tall brick fence with metal spikes on top and the big iron gate was locked by Madame Elise at ten-thirty sharp. She was a formidable woman, feared by all.

One night, there was a very elegant ball in the garden of one of the rich houses. We climbed on a fence to see the festivities until a servant shooed us away. I then decided I will never be a poor outsider, ever. I will fight to get what I want. I will never sit on a fence and watch the more privileged ones.

I was intoxicated by my newfound freedom. I stayed out too late and had to climb the wall frequently. Once, walking back from the Metro late at night a man and a woman in a car accosted me. They were both naked and asked me to join them! I did a marathon sprint to the hostel! As I vaulted over the wall I fell into Madame Elise's arms. She asked me to find other accommodations. I found a roommate, Jacqueline, also from the hostel, and we went house hunting.

We found two tiny rooms to rent in Rue Lafayette behind the Paris Opera. It was owned by a lecherous old man. He said he would rent us the rooms, providing Jacqueline and I would be *"nice"* to him. *"Sure,"* we said, *"we are always very nice."* The

Ole Jepsen

rooms were at the back of a big apartment building. The back rooms had a separate servants' staircase. We were on the sixth floor walk up. The rooms overlooked the roofs of Paris and we had a great view from the skylights. There was no running water except a cold-water tap at the end of a long corridor and the shared toilet was a cubicle with a hole in the floor. You had to lean in to flush to keep your shoes dry. To us, however, this was heaven. Our own rooms with no curfew! Monsieur Du Pont, the landlord, would come wheezing up six floors several times a week and scratch at our locked door. *"Je veux seulement toucher"* (I only want to touch), he would wail much to our amusement. Laughing, we threatened to tell his wife, so after a few weeks he stopped.

Ole Jepsen, with whom I corresponded all this time, invited me to Copenhagen to meet his family. I scraped together the money and arrived very much in love. We got engaged and I was received with much love by his parents, brother, and friends. His father was a very distinguished diplomat who frequently had meetings with his friend the king. They lived in a beautiful house. One evening, we were all in the living room listening to a recording of Mozart's "Eine Kleine Nachtmusic" when Ole stretched out on the carpet in front of the fireplace.

I don't know what possessed me, but I said, "You are going to need an awfully long coffin." I don't think his parents appreciated me after that!

Engagement to Ole

Ole was a planner. He would finish medical school, we would get married, have one child a year and a half later, and a second two years after that. He would become a country doctor and I would have afternoon teas with the vicar and other local dignitaries.

He would not make love to me because he had gotten a prior girlfriend pregnant. Her abortion was very traumatic for both of them. So he snuck into my room every night to just hug me and chat. Later, he visited me in Paris and we still hugged and chatted. Hugging and chatting was getting to be a bit frustrating. I loved this boy, but the chastity thing was getting me down.

At this time I met George Vianes, nineteen, the son of the old Comptroller of Finances in Vietnam when it was a French colony. He was studying at an elite

Georges Vianes

university and was looking forward to a great future. Georges was what the French call of a *"bonne famille"* (a good family). They were very snobbish. You don't get invited to a French home unless you are engaged to a son or daughter, and then only to try and talk you out of it. I fell passionately in love with Georges who was very sexy, adventurous, and uninhibited. He taught me everything there was to know about love. I sent the ring back to Ole in Copenhagen.

I was very poor. My parents struggled to send me money from Israel. It had to be through some shady people due to Israel's currency restrictions. Every month I would go to the old Jewish quarter to get my money from an old Orthodox man. One time he tried to show me pornographic photos. I threatened to tell his Rabbi. When the money came I would take a taxi to a good restaurant and eat a great meal. This made me feel less poor and less hungry for the rest of the month. I was always hungry. When I babysat families never invited me back because I ate anything I could

George and I

find. I started hanging out outside the American Express office near the Opera hoping to meet Americans who needed translating or babysitting. Most of the time, because I was pretty and young, male tourists would try to chat me up. Next door was a restaurant called "Pam Pam," where they would invariably invite me for a bite. There was a back exit behind the restrooms and after I finished eating I would go to "powder my nose," out the back door, and run like hell. I still don't feel guilty about this. After all, they expected favors in return for a meal. I felt that having my company during lunch was payment enough. I did this rarely. I didn't want to run into the same lunch partners, just in case.

I was still friendly with Madame Elise who would send me to baby sit when they needed an English speaker. One day, she sent me over to the Ritz. I was greeted by Harry Winston, the famous jeweler from New York. He was a short rotund man in his sixties and, as many powerful and successful men, he spoke softly. I was introduced to his very distinguished wife, who looked like a more mature Jennifer Jones, and his two sons, aged sixteen and thirteen. I was to entertain and take them around Paris for a week. The boys were great, especially Bruce, the younger of the two. Bruce looked a lot like his dad, had braces, and had an infectious smile. I can't remember the older boy's name—he looked more like his mother and was a great kid too. Mr. Winston gave a hundred dollars a day—a small fortune by my standards—and another hundred per day to feed and entertain the boys! We went everywhere and I ate and ate and ate. Bruce wanted to know if I always ate so much. Life was good. They came several times a year for a few days at a time. I started looking forward to seeing the boys. One day I got a call to go to the Ritz, but when I got there Mr. Winston was alone. He wanted to discuss a proposition with me. He sat me down and explained that he wanted me to be his girlfriend whom he would see when in Paris, without his wife or kids. For sleeping with him a few times a year, I would have a nice apartment, car, and plenty of money to live on. I wouldn't have to work, just study whatever I wanted to. He felt I had a great future at whatever I decided on to do with my life. Of course, I would be sworn to secrecy. I was surprised but somehow not shocked or offended. It was very much a business proposition. There was no groping or disrespect. He was a gentleman. I asked to go home and think about it till the next day. I went home and spent the night with Georges. I did not discuss it with him, but made up my mind.

The next day, I told Mr. Winston I couldn't do it because he was older than me and I didn't fancy him. What I didn't tell him is that I was repulsed by his crepey hands covered in liver spots and the thought of being touched by him made me sick. I also liked his wife. Besides, I told him I had a very serious boyfriend. Mr. Winston was very kind and not at all angry. I asked him why he would need someone when he had such a lovely wife. He explained that older men feel rejuvenated by being with a young girl. He had more than desire for me—he also respected me. Then he asked if I needed money. I told him I needed money for paint to make my maid's room look like Van Gogh's room. He gave me the money and handed me a scruffy paper bag. He wrote down an address and asked me to take a cab and deliver the bag to a Mr. Levy. In the cab, I looked inside the bag. I was shocked! It contained a necklace, bracelet, and earrings set with exquisite diamonds and huge emeralds. They must have been worth an absolute fortune! After I delivered it to Mr. Levy I called Mr. Winston. I asked him why he trusted

me with a fortune in jewels. He explained that it was the safest way to deliver the stuff. No one would possibly imagine I had anything of value in that scruffy paper bag. Besides, he said he trusted me, and, what's more, there was no way someone like me would have the faintest idea how to

Outside Dior in Paris

dispose of such enormous stones. He thanked me and we said goodbye. I never heard from Harry Winston again.

So now I was to go work for Dior! I didn't even know where to start. Madame Elise found a babysitting job for me at the home of a man who worked at Dior's offices. He in turn gave me the name of the man who was in charge of personnel.

The Dior House was a very elegant building in Avenue Montaigne and consisted of a boutique with a separate entrance and doors for the customers, office staff, and workers. Dressed in my finest garments, I presented myself at the gate only to be turned away rudely by an imperious doorman.

The next day, I said I had an appointment with Monsieur Legres, head of personnel, and I was led to a central hall with some armchairs and doors with names on them. I waited until I saw a balding man exit his office. "Monsieur Legres, can I have a word?" I said in my carefully rehearsed schoolgirl French. He looked me up and down speculatively. I have seen that look since I matured and realized my looks could open doors for me. He sat me down and got behind a big desk, but after finding out that I had no work visa he told me categorically to go away. There was no way I could work there in any capacity.

For the next two weeks I went every day and sat outside his office. Whenever he came out to go to lunch or the bathroom, I ran after him begging him to help me. As I was not doing anything criminal, he did not call the police to remove me and I finally wore him down. He agreed to let me work but not get paid. Officially I didn't exist.

Dior had eighteen hundred employees. Aside from offices, showrooms, stock rooms, dining rooms, and design rooms, there were eighteen workrooms (ateliers) each with fifty or more seamstresses. I ended up in Mademoiselle Ginette's atelier. There was a strict pecking order. Mademoiselle Ginette, a dry brittle woman in her forties, was the one to liaise with the design room and ruled her atelier with an iron fist. She was the "Premiere," and had a "Seconde," who took over when she went to lunch or to the design room. We were not allowed to talk during work and Mademoiselle Ginette was a real bitch. She would make sarcastic remarks and enjoyed making the girls cry. When she found out I was Israeli she called me "la petite juive" (little Jewess), and sometimes if I displeased her "sale petite juive" (dirty little Jewess). No one dared stand up to her. Her word was law.

All employees wore white coats including Dior. I suppose it was some attempt at treating everyone as equals. I was constantly getting into trouble exploring during my break. The white coat made me blend in. I discovered that Dior employed scores of very beautiful young men in the design department who didn't wear white coats. I did my hair and thought I looked my best when I realized not one of these beautiful boys even noticed me. I talked about this with the doorman who by now was always very friendly to me. He roared with laughter and explained the boys were all gay and he was one of the few "real" men at Dior.

Dior, who was gay and in a long-term monogamous relationship, liked having beautiful boys around him. Truthfully, the best fashion designers were, and still are to this day, gay men. Perhaps it is the mixture of male and female sensibilities that creates great fashion. The majority of gay men also tend to have superb taste.

Christian Dior

Monsieur Dior was a meek, nondescript, soft-spoken man in his fifties. Rotund, short, and slightly balding, he looked like a little grocer. The first time I saw him I didn't even know who he was. I was waiting for the elevator next to a man in a white coat. When the elevator doors opened there was only room for one. He graciously gave me the place and waited for the next elevator. Once the doors to the elevator closed the other passengers told me who he was. I was shocked!

I was sewing in the atelier and realized the perfection that was demanded. Every garment was lined with very thin silk muslin before it was assembled and lined again with a color-coordinated silk. All visible seams were trimmed with lace. You had to make sure the dress looked as good inside as outside. The more frequent customers had their own made-to-measure mannequins, which were adjusted as the client lost or gained weight. Every garment was fitted live at least twice, and then was delivered in a huge box packed with tissue paper bearing the Dior name. I have never seen so much luxury. Dior loved the scent of lily of the valley, and the whole establishment was suffused with this perfume he called "Diorissimo".

I had been at Dior for several months, when I followed Mademoiselle Ginette. She went to try on one of the new styles in the design room. She didn't know I was behind her as she entered Dior's atelier. It was a huge room with large windows, mirrored walls, and bolts of fabric strewn everywhere. The carpet was a pale grey. The walls white and the room smelled like lily of the valley. Monsieur Dior was sitting on a large throne like antique chair, pointing with a long, thin golden rod, at details on a dress worn by a beautiful model girl.

I am enthralled—almost as if I am in the presence of a superior being, Dior, my hero. I am cowering in a corner when he spots me. "Who are you Mademoiselle?" he asks. I mutter my name as Mademoiselle Ginnette begins pushing me out of the room. "Wait!" says Dior. "Let the child answer." What would you like to do here?" "To work as your assistant," I say emboldened by his kind interest. Mademoiselle Ginette looks on shocked. "I am going to Italy for two weeks. By the time I come back I want to see twenty designs from you, and we shall see what you can do," says Monsieur Dior.

I worked feverishly, day and night. I did my best designs and felt that my great chance was coming. A few days before he was due back, Dior died in Italy. They brought his body back. At his funeral, seeing his casket covered by a mass of lily of the valley, I probably cried harder than anyone else. I was totally devastated. Who knows what direction my life would have taken had he lived? Would he have told me to find another career or would I have become a great designer under his tutelage? What if? What if? I will always wonder.

After Dior died Yves Saint Laurent, one of Dior's pretty boys, took over. He was only nineteen and very talented, but also very nasty. He was mean to everyone. I quit and went full-time to the *"Ecole De La Chambre Syndicale De La Couture Parisienne,"* the best fashion school in France. I learned a lot—they even had us design garments inspired by famous painters such as Braque, Modigliani, or Picasso. Miss Rosie's history of art lessons came in handy.

In the afternoons, I went to the Sorbonne and studied "French Culture and Literature." Unlike the English, the French are jealous of their vast culture. They don't share it readily, and unless you speak good French they have no time for you. I became a total Francophile while in Paris. I could not imagine living anywhere else in the world. I fell in love with everything French. Paris is such a beautiful city—so full of art and history. One never tires of it. I took hour-long walks just exploring this wondrous city, breathing in the atmosphere with every breath of air. I was intoxicated by Paris, the city I could never leave.

In August, Paris shuts down and everyone heads south to the sea. Georges was on vacation and went to St. Tropez with friends. When my schools closed for vacation, I acquired a Vespa that had seen better days. It had no brakes, but I somehow managed to navigate down to St.Tropez where it finally died and I had to abandon it. We spent an idyllic vacation living very frugally—five to a room and sleeping on straw mattresses on the floor—but when you are young and in love you live on soft clouds. We stared at the rich on their massive yachts and happily paddled our little air mattress.

One of us would go to a fancy restaurant and sit by an open window. The bread from the breadbasket would get handed out, and so would butter and olives. After eating half the food, a dead fly would be smuggled in through the window and the waiter would be called over. With great apologies, a fresh dish would be brought in, which would also find its way out. When it came to paying, the meal was generally free. We all had a marvelous vacation. I was in love. The future looked sunny, endless, and full of possibilities.

France took in a lot of refugees following the 1956 Hungarian Revolution. I decided to help these brave people as a translator. The first day there, I realized these people by and large were pretty obnoxious and demanding. They were complaining and criticizing, impatient, rude, and totally unappreciative of anything the French government generously gave them. I quit in disgust.

Back in Paris, Georges took me to see plays at the Comedie Francaise. It was wonderful to see Moliere or Racine in the original language and understand it well. I read feverishly, poems by Baudelaire, books from Maupassant to Camus, and went to the Opera. At first I didn't like it very much, but since then, I have become Opera mad. Listening to Opera has provided me with endless joy.

I could now understand why the Hungarian lady cried when she returned to the Paris of her youth. Every day I discovered beautiful parts of the city, so full of history. I spent time in museums and art galleries. My mind was filled with knowledge, culture, and beauty.

Time came for me to return to Israel to do my military service. They would not grant me an extension. I had to start planning to leave my beloved Paris. I was in total shock to discover I was pregnant. My stepfather came over to deal with it. I went to meet him at the train coming in from Marseilles. When I saw him coming towards me, I suddenly realized how old he had become. I think I grew up that day—I became the strong adult. Needless to say, he was not very happy with me.

Finally, we were invited to dinner at George's parents' apartment. The elegant dining room was all dark walls and dark wood. The conversation was also dark and very strained. We had Coq-au-Vin and a much-discussed bottle of wine. George's older brother Pierre was there. He was a very hostile and angry man, virtually accusing me of getting pregnant on purpose to ensnare his brother. I knew he was an avowed anti-Semite, very much against George marrying me. When he said I was acting "Jewish" I got up and left with my father. Georges did not try to stop me or talk to me the next day. We flew back to Israel. I was devastated. Not only did I lose Georges but also my beloved Paris. How could I possibly go on living?

IV.
ISRAEL AGAIN

Back in Tel-Aviv it was decided that I would have an abortion. I was barely nineteen. There was no way I could support a child—a fatherless one at that. The baby would have no future. It was still very sad. I went to the gynecologist accompanied by my mother's housekeeper. Mother couldn't face it. I was asleep for the procedure and woke up in a different recovery room. As I opened my eyes I saw a picture on the opposite wall. It was "Two Tahitian Women" by Gauguin. That same picture hung above my bed in Paris. Georges had given it to me saying the girl on the left reminded him of me.

I cried for a long time—for the baby, for Georges who let me go, for my loneliness, for Paris. Later I found out that Georges' nasty anti-Semitic brother,

Pierre, that respectable married father of two children, ran away with a gay man. What a hypocrite!

I went to the army offices to enlist and failed my IQ test. My Hebrew was so poor I messed it up completely. So they deferred me again. I felt I was a stranger in a strange land and very homesick for Paris.

Tomi started taking me out and got me a job writing a women's page for the paper called *"Uj Kelet."* At this time of heavy immigration there were enough newcomers to support a daily paper in Hungarian. I really enjoyed researching and writing my weekly column.

"Two Tahitian Women" by Gauguin

The editor was a charming older gentleman from Budapest where he had edited a very important paper before the war. During my tenure on the paper, I found out he had a long-term affair with an intellectual Hungarian lady who was pressing him to leave his wife.

In her hopeless despair, she took an overdose of sleeping pills before he was due to arrive at her apartment. She was unconscious when he found her. A letter addressed to him explained she did not want to live in these conditions and asked him not to try and save her. He took the letter and quietly left the apartment. He could not leave his wife because they met coming back from the camps where she lost two children. She was very fragile and he was the only thing left in her life. Though they were intellectually unsuited he did not have the strength to leave her. He loved his mistress, but he quietly closed the door and let her die. He died a year later, I am sure of a broken heart.

With Tomi at a ball

One has no right to pass judgment on people so damaged by what happened to them. I knew all three of them. They were all good people. They were all victims. In my youth I met so many people who shuffled throughout their lives, permanently damaged by the horrors they survived.

By this time, Tomi was working for the biggest daily paper in Israel. He took me to many performances and important social events. He even had me accompany him to interview important people. I got to see and hear Yves Montand, Juliette Greco, Margot Fontaine, and went to scores of wonderful concerts conducted and performed by the world's finest artists. I met countless famous writers, actors, and musicians. In those days everyone came to perform in Israel and marvel at what the little country was able to achieve. It was a period of enormous enthusiasm and hope for the future. We were building utopia.

Tomi took me to dances too. At a students' ball I was elected beauty queen. After several other similar experiences, Tomi suggested I try for the Miss Israel title. If elected, I would not only get prize money, but I would get to travel to Europe and to the United States to fundraise for Israel. The pageant was run by Israel's largest women's weekly magazine. I made it to the top ten when I was called to talk to the organizers. They explained that Miss Israel had to be fluent in several languages, especially English, and be a worthy representative of the country. They felt that intellectually I was what they wanted and had no doubt I would meet the beauty criteria. They asked me to wear a red evening gown for the final pageant. I was terribly excited! I was going to be Miss Israel. I'd travel, see the world, and who knows what would happen in the future?!

The beautiful long red satin dress my mother made me is hanging on the wall opposite my bed in my room. I close my eyes and imagine the triumph of getting the Miss Israel title and crown. I can feel the crown on my head. I will travel, see the world, live in luxury hotels, and meet lots of fascinating people. The world is opening up to me. I can hardly sleep from the excitement.

Three days before the pageant I was thrown out of the event! The rules in Israel were very strict about who was considered to be a Jew. A child is considered Jewish if her mother is Jewish. My mother had converted to Judaism through a progressive reform synagogue, so the organizers decided I was not a Jew. Hitler considered me to be a Jew and my father died in Auschwitz, but in Israel I was not Jewish. How could a non-Jewish Miss Israel represent her country? I was devastated. Not only were my dreams shattered but also prejudice raised its ugly head again! The nasty fundamentalist Rabbis of Israel still have influence in too many matters in Israel. Yet their power has diminished since Tomi became minister of justice. His main focus was to diminish the stranglehold on the religious right.

I was now stuck, not knowing what to do with my future. I didn't want to work for my mother. There was really no job there for me, and so I began modeling again. I was quite successful, but it gave me no satisfaction. Tomi still took me to glamorous places and interesting interviews and the gossip columns were full of photos and mentions of the *"Naarat Hazohar," "The Golden Girl,"* and *"The Glamour Girl."*

Tomi and I were talking about marriage, but his mother didn't like me and probably hoped for a better match for him. He was now writing for the biggest daily in Israel and had a great future. My stepfather in his wisdom predicted Tomi had no future—just as before he predicted that Ole in Copenhagen and Georges in Paris had no future either. The man had a real talent at predictions. Ole now owns two hospitals, Georges became the youngest Judge in Paris, and Tomi, after a distinguished journalistic career, became head of Israeli Television, leader of a major political party, Member of Parliament, Minister of Justice, and Deputy Prime Minister.

Tomi married Shula, the daughter of an editor of *"Maariv,"* the important daily paper he worked for. His mother was right. I would have been the wrong person for his needs. I am selfish and ambitious—a not very good wife material. I think he made the right choice. His wife is a wonderful person and a very talented writer. She bore him three wonderful, talented children. We became good friends and walked our first children in the park together. Shula and I are still friends.

When I lose someone I loved, I write to them, it eases the grief and somehow adds to their memory...

Dear Tomi,

You always called me Katika. You called me that the last time we spoke on the phone. You always called me Katika with such affection and sweetness in your voice. It always meant so much to me and now I will never hear it again. Now that you are gone will everything you meant to so many people be forgotten? Will you become a footnote in Israeli history books, your writings lost in archives, your wisdom extinguished, your intellect gone?

We loved each other once. It seems centuries ago. We were both so young then. Our parents were typical of their generation—families cobbled together from remains of the Holocaust. Everyone lost someone they loved and then somehow settled with other wounded beings, raised children together, and even derived a modicum of joy and happiness.

I remember coming to your apartment with my parents. It was a modest place with lots of brown furniture. Your mother was very beautiful. I met you there. I was thirteen and you were twenty-one. You came and took me out the next day. We went to the cinema on your big black motorbike. I was so excited. I wore my blue dress with the little white dots and you had a crisp white shirt. On the way home we went through a quiet shuttered market area near the central bus station. You stopped for a moment. You said you wanted to show me something. It was the first time I was kissed—there, against the metal shutter in the doorway of a shop. I was quite shocked. I didn't know people kissed with their tongue. It was thrilling and strange, pleasant and scary. I remember asking to go home and not being able to fall asleep from the thrill of it all. I developed a serious crush on you but obviously I was too young and you moved on. You were a journalist for the Hungarian daily paper "Uj Kelet" and started writing for other papers as well.

When I went to study in Paris, you wrote me a letter saying that you were debating studying law or just sticking with journalism. I remember urging you to study law. You could do journalism on the side and law would be handy in politics. I was certain you would be running the country someday. After I came back from Paris, we continued our relationship. I was now all grown up, elegant, sophisticated, and no longer frightened by a kiss. You started to take me out to glamorous parties, concerts, plays, and to interviews with famous people. You were so proud of me and you made me feel like the most beautiful woman in the world. I became, once again, very much in love with you. You loved me too and we started to talk about marriage. You were very jealous, to the point that you made me sit with my back to the entrance in cafes so I would only have eyes for you. I became known as the "Golden Girl" and we were in the newspapers all the time. You took me everywhere. We went to fabulous concerts, plays, and your interviews with world leaders and artists. I learned so much from you.

When I fled to New York it was a very sad part of my life followed. My marriage was over. I was desperately lonely and poor. I lost my identity. I became nobody. Years later, I found out your beautiful mother, who had remarried and was widowed again, was diagnosed with cancer. When she found out it was terminal, she took her own life. She did not want to go bald and die in pain. I read about you in the papers. Shula gave birth to your son, Yair, and you became editor at "Maariv." Our lives were different and we lost touch for a while.

We met up again in London, where you and Shula lived for a short time when I started working there. We reconnected and having children of the same age we started walking them again in the park on weekends. You tried to persuade me to go back to Israel but I couldn't see how I could make a living to start again. I was scared. You were both so kind and caring.

You then went back to Israel where your career forged ahead. You wrote plays, guidebooks, a type of Michelin guide, became head of Israeli Television, head of a political party, and then Minister of Justice and Deputy Prime Minister. I have often thought of my stepfather's prediction about you having no future. Shula became a successful novelist and you had another daughter, Merav. I eventually married again, Michael Phillips, had a son, Jonathan, and I became a very successful designer in London. I made a lot of money and lived in a beautiful large house in Hampstead. You came to visit and approved. "This is the sort of environment you belong to," you said, but you felt that I should be in Israel. You called me a "national treasure."

I followed your career in the papers. I was sure you would be the next prime minister. I was planning on coming to your inauguration and making a great speech about my stepfather who said *not to marry you because you had no future. You called me, "Katika," you said, "I am coming to Washington D.C. next month. I will have a free day there. Come to see me. Who knows when we'll see each other again?" I flew to Washington and you met me in the lobby of your hotel. It was very emotional. We looked into each other's faces searching for the Tomi and Kati we once knew and loved. But we had become old. I was sixty-six and you were seventy-four. We were both heavier and your hair had turned white. But there was your smile and the way you said "Katika." There I recognized the old Tomi I loved.*

You came to Washington as Deputy Prime Minister to speak the to "AIPAC," the very influential Jewish American group who were great supporters of Israel. We had lunch with Tom Lantos, the very charming Hungarian Senator from California. Although he was in his seventies he was still very handsome and had a twinkle in his eye. He hid with you in Budapest during the Holocaust. You were children together and friends for life. I was awed by being treated as an equal in the company of such great men. Unfortunately, Tom Lantos died of cancer too, a short time before you.

We went in a bulletproof vehicle surrounded by your bodyguards to the Smithsonian and then to the Hirshorn Museum. We were treated like royalty, squired around by the directors in virtual privacy. In the evening, you and your bodyguards picked me up and took us to a Chinese restaurant. You always loved Chinese food. We ate surrounded by two tables where the bodyguards sat. They were all lawyers from your ministry of justice office doing double duty. Remember I asked you if you were frightened by the possibility of an assassination attempt. "Why should I?" you replied, "I've already lived." We had a long dinner. We talked for hours. The next day you were back to work, seeing the President and other dignitaries. I looked at you, held your hand, and hugged you. "Goodbye, old friend. I love you." That was the last time we met.

The next morning I went to the "AIPAC" conference to hear you speak. There were thousands of people and security was tight. I sat down and watched you on stage. The huge screens allowed me to see your every expression. When you started to speak you could hear a pin drop. I can almost remember verbatim what you said:

"After my father, a prominent lawyer in our town, was deported, my beautiful mother and I fled to Budapest. We hid in a Wallenberg house. Wallenberg was a Swedish diplomat who bought several houses in Budapest, put them under Swedish Diplomatic protectorate. More than a hundred thousand Jews took refuge in those houses. Wallenberg was a real hero who unfortunately was captured by the invading Soviets and executed in Russia. Conditions for my mother and me while we hid were bad. We had very little food and not much heat. It was very crowded in that basement. As people started dying they were taken and left in the attic. Soon there were more people in the attic than in the basement. At one point, they cut off the water and the stench became overwhelming. I was thirteen and my mother arranged for me to have my Bar Mitzvah there in the basement. Before the ceremony she pulled out a bottle of perfume, Chanel 5. She smashed it spilling its contents all over the floor." My son will not have his Bar-Mitzvah in a place stinking of shit," she said. I still love that perfume, Channel 5.

Bombs were falling. Things got more chaotic and the Hungarian Nazi sympathizers broke in and arrested all of us. They were marching us to the Danube. There, they would tied groups of Jews together with wire and shoot every third person to save bullets. The dead would fall into the river and drag the living to a watery death. They stood no chance. As we passed an outdoor urinal my mother dragged me in and told me to pee. "But I don't need to," I cried. "Never mind, just pee!" she hissed. Suddenly a plane started to strafe the area. Everybody fled and there we stood. We were hidden in the urinal. I stood there, up to my ankles in snow, freezing, crying, frightened. I have since traveled all over the world and seen huge empty lands everywhere, but on that day there was no place for a thirteen-year-old Jewish child to hide. In the whole big world, there was no place for him, and this is why Israel must survive!

The audience of several thousands erupted in a cheer that shook the building. There was not a dry eye and several people were openly sobbing. I decided to leave and got a cab to take me to the Holocaust Museum. In front of the hall I saw three orthodox Jews in full regalia, beards, long black coats, and big fur trimmed hats. They held signs demonstrating against Israel. "Israel has no right to exist" and "The Messiah hasn't come. There is no Israel." I stopped the cab and jumped out. In those moments when I am totally enraged, I don't think. I just act and I ran towards the demonstrators. I think I wanted to kill them. I tried to grab the nearest one but because I am a woman and my touch is forbidden, all three men turned tail and ran away. I ran after them screaming at them when suddenly I felt someone grab me from behind. It was my Ethiopian cab driver! "Lady," he said, "Be careful. They could arrest you and get you deported!" Hearing my accent he thought I was an immigrant too and wanted to protect me.

Yes Tomi, I understand your crusade against the religious fanatics. I hate them too, no matter what religion they profess. You tried to protect Israel from them. You were my great white hope to save our people. Unfortunately you lost your clout, your party is out of Parliament, and I am frightened for the future. I am frightened for the soul of Israel.

A few weeks before you died, you told me you had cancer but said it was okay. It was in remission. We didn't talk long because the Prime Minister was calling you on another line. We never talked again. Now you are dead, and I will no longer hear "Katika" with so much affection and sweetness and love in your voice. I will miss you and mourn you forever.

Tomi died in June of 2008.

Their eldest daughter died tragically. When I saw Tomi later the light seemed to have gone out of his eyes. I always think of Tomi as the king in the story, with one eye that laughs and one eye that cries.

My stepfather decided to find me a rich husband. Being insecure, I think money was the most important thing for him. There was a succession of rich boys and men from remote places—mainly in South America—who came to Israel to find a nice Jewish girl to marry. I met some to please my father, but I had no intention to even consider any of them. The final straw was the little bald guy who was waiting for me on the living room sofa one day. He was so small, his little feet didn't reach the floor, but he had a big yacht and millions. That was it! After that, every time I was introduced to one of these poor men, I would act obnoxiously. I'd stutter, pick my nose, chew loudly with my mouth open,

Yoram and I

scratch my bottom, or say totally inappropriate things. Finally, my parents gave up on me and stopped trying to sell me.

Gertie, Mother, and Yoram

One evening during Purim (the Jewish Halloween) Tomi and I went to get a sandwich before a party. I was dressed as a witch in black leotards with a black cone hat and carried a broom. My hair was long, spread out over my shoulders and the cape on by back. There was a man at the counter who didn't take his eyes off me. Turning to Tomi he asked, *"Aren't you going to introduce me to your beautiful witch?"* Tomi reluctantly introduced me to Yoram Matmor, 33 years old, a penniless writer. I was smitten! He was not what you would call handsome but he made up for it with wit and

The Sternheims,
Yoram's parents

Yoram's father,
1916, In the Austro-
Hungarian army

charisma. He had an interesting face and beautiful green eyes that could look deep into my soul. Yoram was very intelligent and well read. He was born in Timişoara, a town about an hour from Nagyvarad. His parents, the Sternheims, had been very wealthy before the war. They traveled a lot, dressed for dinner, and Yoram's mother was a world-class beauty. His father owned a big textile factory and doted on his family. Hansi (as Yoram was called then) had been eight and his little sister Gertie four when their mother died of cancer. His desperate father remarried five years later and his new wife couldn't cope with the boy. The final straw was when his stepmother found him reading a racy book out loud to the maid and the cook in the kitchen

Timişoara was in Romania, but fearing the Nazis they decided to ship the boy to Palestine, to his uncle. The boy arrived in Haifa looking like he was going on safari, wearing a pith helmet on his head. His uncle, a sweet and kind man, was married to a very strong, mean wife. They had two daughters, fifteen and sixteen, and they all lived in a small apartment in Jerusalem. The uncle was an unsuccessful entrepreneur who barely made enough money, and an extra mouth to feed was much resented by his wife. Yoram started school and did well. He changed Hansi Sternheim to a more acceptable Hebrew Yoram Matmor, and, having a talent for languages, he soon spoke good Hebrew.

Yoram in the
British Navy

The wheel came off when they found out there was something going on between Yoram and the older girl. It was never clear who did what or who started it. Despite the uncle's protest Yoram was sent to a boarding school. At sixteen he ran away to Egypt. He lied about his age he joined the British Navy. He matured among rough sailors and by the time he was seventeen he spoke perfect English and knew every bawdy English song in the world. He was dragged through the seedy brothels of Alexandria, learned to drink like a sailor, and became a life-long Anglophile. During all this time he read and read voraciously—anything he could lay his hands on. By now, he spoke Hungarian, Romanian, German, French, Hebrew, and English. So the Navy decided to make him a translator of Italian. "But Sir," he protested," I don't speak Italian." The officer in charge replied, "Don't worry about it. Just shout louder. They'll get the meaning of it." So Yoram became a translator. The prisoners taught him Italian. He was eventually reassigned because he was too friendly with the prisoners. He was put in charge of keeping track of supplies. After counting tanks going into a warehouse and missing one coming out at the other end, he was placed on painting duty. This consisted of painting a ship from one end and by the time he got to the other end it was time to start again. He went AWOL and joined the Haganah, the fledgling Israeli army.

When the UN sanctioned the establishment of the state of Israel there was great jubilation. What a great historic moment that must have been, especially for the wretched survivors of the camps who managed to get into Palestine through the blockades. There would be no more "subhuman Jews." When the UN recognized the State of Israel all the surrounding countries attacked. Yoram was put in charge of a group of newly arrived Romanian immigrants who were drafted and didn't know a word of Hebrew. Because they couldn't understand commands, they wandered merrily into a group of Arab gunners. The Arabs fled thinking that if the enemy just walks around casually, all is lost. Yoram who was trying to catch up with them was promoted for bravery. During the house-to-house battle for Jerusalem, Yoram found a chocolate bar which he was savoring. A huge famished Great Dane snatched it out of his hand. The poor dog decided Yoram was his new master and followed him around sharing his food until the end of the war when he finally found him a home on a Kibbutz.

There were a lot of casualties, many of them camp survivors. As a Jew, it is better to die on your feet than on your knees. An era of hope and optimism followed. Never again will we get killed. We now had a home in which a new utopia will be created!

Yoram went to university and studied philosophy under the great Martin Buber partly because classes were in the afternoon and Yoram hated getting up in the morning. He read extensively, mostly books in their original languages. He was the most educated man I ever met. He also started acting and writing, being called a "promising young writer" in the newspapers.

Yoram was very poor, but he wooed me with red roses. I fell in love, a love different to any other. He was my soul mate, my teacher, and my mentor. It went beyond sexual passion. It was a deep spiritual connection. I wonder if being from similar backgrounds as children had something to do with it? I never had to explain myself. He knew my mind instinctively, understood me, and tried to eradicate flaws in my character. He taught me, not to envy, not to be petty, but to respect people even if they were my enemies, and, above all, to develop my brain. At one point,

Yoram Matmor

I toyed with the idea of becoming an flight attendant. He screamed at me, "You are not entitled to ignore your intellect to become a flying waitress. Read! Think!"

He gave me books to read and would discuss them with me. He taught me politics and general knowledge. It was as if I had become his greatest creation. He taught me to write, to speak, and to stand up for myself, not to be shy, not to be easily flattered, and to aspire to a greater understanding of human nature. Above all, I loved his fine brain, which never ceased to amaze me.

I, Yoram, my stepfather, Yoram's father (far right)

When I announced to my parents that I was very serious about Yoram, my stepfather threw me out. So I moved into Yoram's rented room with the lumpy straw mattress. The gossip columns were full of our story and we were invited everywhere. Everyone loves a good romance.

Newspaper clipping,
Wedding, 1959

Newspaper clipping
Before wedding, 1959

We got married in the garden of a small house we rented. I had to go to a ritual bath called a "Mikveh" to prove I was Jewish or the Rabbi would not consent to marry us. Religious marriage was the only legal union in Israel. I was photographed coming out of the Mikveh and the wedding made all the papers. I got married in an old white cocktail dress I had and we did the catering ourselves. My parents finally agreed to come to the wedding, but they arrived late. My stepfather said, *"I'll be on time for the next one."* He was.

It was a great, loud, joyous wedding. We were all poor and happy and we were building a better world. Our country would be built on peace and human values. There would be a wonderful new world for us and our children. These months were some of the happiest of my life. With Yoram, who was fourteen years older than me, I recaptured some of the security I lost when my father went away. The future was rosy.

Yoram's Nobel prize would follow I was sure. No one in the world was a better writer. So what if we barely had enough to pay the rent. Poverty was always a temporary state with me and living with a genius was so exhilarating.

The bride, 1959

The movie *"Exodus"* was being shot in Israel. I went to try and get a small part, playing a hungry young mother on a ship that tried to land in Israel. Otto Preminger, the director, took one look at me and screamed at his assistant director, "Sind sie verucht?" (Are you crazy?). Apparently I looked neither Jewish nor hungry, and reminded him of the star of the film. I cried bitterly. The money would have bought us a big refrigerator, which we really needed. Yoram made ends meet writing skits for the various army theatres and I had a small income from the woman's page I was writing for the Hungarian *"Uj Kelet."*

I decided to try for something bigger and went to see the deputy editor at *"Maariv,"* the biggest Israeli daily. The man received me kindly and I sold him on a weekly woman's page, which the paper didn't have. He told me I was also allowed to write a weekly article for this page on any subject of my choice. This was a fantastic opportunity for a twenty-year-old and I almost fainted with joy. When he asked me how much I wanted to be paid I asked for what I thought was a reasonable sum. He agreed and then taught me a lesson I have never forgotten.

"Never name your price in a negotiation. If I were to offer you too little you could have asked for more. However, you named your price, which I shall pay. But, you see, I would have offered you double that. Never forget that sometimes people think you are worth more than what you believe."

As a journalist

My column was a huge success. I made friends with female journalists from other papers. We often covered the same stories and when there was nothing to cover we wrote articles about each other. I also did interviews with famous women and did my weekly article on various subjects. Yoram taught me to write, and was my discerning critic. We became regular friends with Tomi and his wife and the humorist Ephraim Kishon and his wife. The brilliant cartoonist Dosh and his wife were in the group also. Interestingly, everyone except Kishon's wife was of Hungarian Jewish origins. If Hitler had his way none of us would have been alive. During this period the Kishons, Yoram, and I made a small comic amateur movie about adultery. Being shy, I insisted on wearing a sweater under my sexy revealing

With Dani, 1959

nightgown. I have begged the Kishons for a copy. They are both dead now, so I will not be able to show this movie to my grandchildren.

One of our friends was Atallah Mansour, a wonderful Arab journalist. He became a very close friend and spent time at our house. He sometimes lent us money when we were short. We were continuously short of money.

As I became more and more successful Yoram was writing less and less. When commissioned to write for the army, he would smuggle a novel into his workroom and read for hours. He started missing deadlines.

I was pregnant with my first son Dani. We named him after the hero in Yoram's most controversial play called "Machaze Ragil" (A Usual Performance). It is a play about a young man Dani who is played by a piece of wood. His destiny is determined by his parents, teachers, the army and his country, without any input from him. It is an anti-war play, not popular in those days.

I believed in equality and decided that what was good enough for the poor was good enough for me. I went into labor at seven in the morning at the *"Hakirya"* hospital in a big birthing room with twenty beds. To my disappointment I learned that childbirth does not observe the first-come-first-served rule. Women came and went, and I was still in labor in the evening. My nine-and-a half-pound breach baby should have been delivered by Caesarian section, but the lone doctor in attendance thought otherwise.

It was a hot October day and time moved slowly. I was in agony and exhausted. They brought a bunch of medical students to look at me. A man walked past with a broom. It got dark and still nothing. A nurse walked by and told me the baby's bottom was out and he was a boy, but it was seven in the evening before the whole baby came out. He was blue and had to be put in an oxygen tent for a few hours. Yoram's father, that sweet gentleman, sat on a wooden bench outside the hospital for twelve hours. He was the only one who never left.

Yoram's Father

Dani was circumcised at home. It is a big event for Jews, a big celebration, and everyone brings presents for the baby. I was very upset handing my baby to a bearded *"Mohel"* (a religious man whose job it is to do this) and when it was over he handed me the foreskin, which I was supposed to bury. Being traumatized and crying, I put it on a small plate, and left it on a bookshelf. Lolita, our pet cat got hold of it and a big chase ensued. Yoram ran down the street yelling, *"Lolita, Lolita! Come here!"* We never recovered the missing foreskin and I used to have nightmares about the cat trying to eat the rest of my baby.

I couldn't breastfeed and we had to learn to make formulas. This was very complicated in those days, with glass bottles, milk powder, and rubber nipples. Everything had to be sterilized in boiling water. When I resumed work, I carried

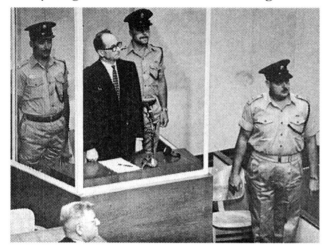

Trail of Adolf Eichmann in Israel

Dani with me in a soft straw basket, which I slung on my shoulder. If I was out during feeding time and had no access to formula I would spoon some tea into him. He seemed to thrive on what would now horrify me as neglect. We took him everywhere, to work, to parties. I resumed my column, writing about babies and children. After all, when we are young we know everything.

Holding Dani in my arms, I listen to Eichman's trial on the radio. Eichman was the man responsible for the deportation of the Hungarian Jews—something he continued to do with zeal even after the Germans began losing the war. He diverted trains from supplying German troops in order to transport the Hungarian Jews to death camps. He was a meek looking family man—extremely ruthless and efficient—a brilliant organizer who fled at the end of the war. He lived under a false name in Argentina. The Israeli secret service, the "Mossad," kidnapped him and brought him to trial in Israel. I listen to the opening words of the historic trial: "The State of Israel against Adolf Eichman for crimes against humanity."

Tears run down my face. I am holding the result of my triumphant survival, my Jewish child. The man who killed my father and all those I knew and loved is now being prosecuted. I feel I am part of history, and cannot stop the tears. It is the most emotional moment of my life.

The trial went on for a long time, with heart wrenching testimonials from witnesses—poor, broken, tortured souls. There was not a shadow of doubt in my mind that Israel was doing the right thing. Throughout the trial, Eichman never showed a flicker of remorse. He kept saying he was "just doing his job." When he was condemned to death by hanging, many of his victims volunteered to push the button that would release the trap door. Three people were chosen randomly. One of them was my editor at "Maariv." There were three people and three buttons, so no one ever knew if he was the one whose button activated the release of the trap door. I am still in awe of the historical enormity of the whole trial and execution. Unfortunately, we did not have television in Israel at this time.

I was hired through my paper by the milk marketing board to find five very fat women and put them on a two-week dairy diet to prove it was a great way to lose weight. I was to take them to a luxury hotel in Jerusalem, where they would meet dignitaries, go shopping, and generally have a wonderful time. I was to

Milk Marketing

weigh them daily and phone the results to my paper in Tel-Aviv to be published. These were all poor women who worked heavy physical jobs. Instead of losing weight, they were gaining about a pound a day on average. The resting and lack of work made the results a big joke. The whole country laughed at us.

Allen Ginsberg

We used to have lots of parties at our house. One morning, after a party, I found a man asleep in our bathtub. He looked at me and asked, "What are you doing here?" He was an actor who became a friend.

None of us had many luxuries so when I acquired a whole Hungarian salami, I invited my friends to come and share it. One of them brought a hairy American writer Allen Ginzberg. When we all went out to the garden to have some lemonade, he stayed in the kitchen. I went back to get the salami, to discover that he had eaten half of it! I was furious and yelled at him. I don't care if he was an icon of the beat generation he was a greedy, rude pig!

During this period the Prime Minister Ben-Gurion was having some difficulties getting his coalition government together, so I tried to help out. I wrote an article advising him to use the theatre tactics I employed when I was a child. Promise everyone the crown until they sign on and then play the king himself. They won't leave—there isn't another theatre to go to. I went to the paper at night, directly to the printing room where everybody assumed my article had been cleared by the editor. When the paper came out I was called by my editor and told off. I was also warned that because of my husband's politically incorrect pacifist leanings, I stood a good chance to be fired from my job. The writing was definitely on the wall. If you are about to be fired—or about to be left by a man—be the first to leave. Take your intact dignity with you. I left the paper.

I decided to have the first "boutique" in Israel. On a main street, called *Dizengoff*, they had a gallery of second floor shops, one of which I rented. I had no money so I borrowed from a usurer, at forty percent, and started making clothes. The workroom was a windowless little attic above the shop with just enough space for a table, some shelves, and two sewing machines. I started designing hip young garments, the sort I would wear, and soon I got quite a following. I was so keen on the designs and the quality of the garments, that the business side was incidental. If a garment cost me ten pounds and I sold it for fifteen, I thought I made five pounds. I didn't take into account the cost of the capital, the fact that I had to carry a large stock of fabrics, and that I lacked the money owed to me—money owed by friends who loved my clothes but who were poor and couldn't pay

enough. The more I sold the more money I needed to borrow and the more money I lost. At the same time, because I was young and enthusiastic, I had no idea as to what would sell. I did the best work of my life. At one point I even started branching out into Men's wear, calling it *"Kati Matmor for Men."* I felt there was nothing I couldn't do.

A succession of various child minders followed because I worked day and night, and Yoram was not the most attentive of fathers. I decided to take a moneyed partner who unfortunately started harassing

At a concert with parents

me sexually and became rather nasty. I kicked him out and once had to call the police to take him away because he was threatening me. He had photos of a naked girl, photographs not showing the girl's head. He started showing them around town, pretending it was of me. It so happens that the woman in the photos had no stretch marks, which I do, but I wasn't about to show my belly around to quell the gossip. I went to see the editor of a sleazy weekly magazine. He was quite an intelligent person who gave me good advice.

"Never give in to slander and blackmail. Pretend the worst has already happened, and take it from there. Bad gossip and publicity is better than not being noticed at all. When you have a business, any publicity is good. People use yesterday's paper to wrap fish in. They forget the gossip but you get name recognition."

I had bought some beautiful expensive Harris Tweed fabric and stored it up in my workroom. One of my model girls asked to borrow the shop keys because she forgot her purse. By some hunch I decided to check the shop. To my horror I found her with a very prominent, old, and famous English philanthropist cavorting on my Harris Tweed which she had spread on the floor! They couldn't go to his hotel because his wife was there. I screamed at them so loudly that people came running. I took pity on them, and hid them until the crowd dispersed, but he sure was a very ugly old man on my beautiful piece of tweed. Now I can never look at tweed without giggling.

Designs for my boutique

We were broke so we had to move to a smaller place, an apartment on a main street. It was small and noisy and I was always exhausted. One morning Dani, who was a toddler, climbed on a chair and opened the front door. Wearing only a vest he went for a walk on the street. The neighbors brought him back. Life was getting harder and harder. We moved again.

I discovered I was pregnant. I decided I couldn't possibly afford another child and made an appointment with my doctor to have the pregnancy terminated. I was reading *"The Last of the Just,"* a great masterpiece by Andre Schwartz-Bart. The book has affected my life and outlook so much. There was no way I was going to abort my Jewish child. I wanted Dani to have a brother or sister, so he wouldn't ever feel as alone in the world as I did.

We moved yet again. The only work I could get was designing for the stage, which didn't pay much. There were lawsuits from creditors. I couldn't handle appearing in court and hid my head under a pillow. I was seven months pregnant and begged Yoram to get a well-paid job in the tin mines of Timnah. *"I am a writer, not a miner,"* he answered. I was too proud and too ashamed to turn to my friends for help. Because I did not appear when summoned, the court issued an arrest warrant for me. Seeing no way out, I begged my parents for a ticket to New York, where they had emigrated two years before.

A police car followed the taxi to the airport. I was convinced they were after me and I sat on the floor of the cab the whole way. I was becoming paranoid. I boarded the plane with Dani, a teddy bear, a record player, and a few clothes in a small bag. As the plane started taxiing, I could hardly see Yoram through my tears. A doctor once told me that a pregnant woman should not sign important documents or be expected to make rational decisions because the hormones drive us slightly crazy. As liberated as I am, I believe he had a point.

We had a layover in Paris and I fell into an exhausted sleep in the waiting room. I woke up seeing Dani on the lap of a stranger, an Arab-looking man. I am sure he was just being nice, but I panicked. As I grabbed the heavy child and started running with him, I felt a gush of blood running down my leg. They took me to some infirmary and told me to rest. I found a phone and dialed the only number I remembered in Paris—my former love, George.

It was one o'clock in the morning when the phone rang in George's parents' house. His father answered and when I asked to speak to George he told me he was away on his honeymoon.

V.
NEW YORK CITY

My parents made me as welcome as they could in New York. They lived in a comfortable one bedroom apartment on the seventeenth floor in *"Lincoln Towers,"* a conglomeration of apartment buildings by the river on the West side of Manhattan. My mother had customers come to the apartment. The living room also served as the fitting room. My stepfather would stay in the bedroom while the fitting went on. When I arrived they gave the bedroom to Dani and me, and slept on a sofa bed in the living room. I now realize, I had a total breakdown. For several days I could not stop crying and wouldn't eat or drink. Then I slept for days and refused to speak to anyone. When I emerged, my stepfather told me that he had been right and I should have listened to him. I went back to sleep for another week.

There were no great news in Israel the week I left, so the story of my flight made front pages in all the papers. The speculations were outlandish. I left because the father of my unborn child was the Ambassador from Gabon, a friend of ours. I left because I was suspect politically. I left because I found a rich American. They papers reported everything but the truth—that I was a seven month pregnant twenty-four year old who couldn't cope and had a breakdown. All my dreams were shattered. I owed about ten thousand dollars, which I didn't know how to repay. I was wanted by the court for not appearing and deeply ashamed. When you fall, it is much harder falling from the top. Now I was all the way down. In New York I became a nobody.

"Why Did Kati Matmor Disappear?"

The local Jewish community rallied to help me. I received baby clothes, a beautiful carriage, changing table, everything I would possibly need. Above all, I got the name of Dr. Gizella Perl, a very prominent gynecologist on Park Avenue. Dr Perl was going to take care of me and deliver my baby for a very nominal fee. Dr. Perl was a Hungarian Jewish middle-aged woman who had the rare gift of vast medical knowledge allied with total compassion. I cried on her shoulder several times.

As the time for my delivery was nearer, the baby had not yet turned. The child was large so Dr. Perl decided to manipulate it by hand. Amazingly, she turned the baby in just a few minutes so he would not be a breech birth. In those days we didn't know the sex of the baby in advance, so I waited excitedly to meet my new child.

I was in the elevator at Macy's department store with

I, pregnant, the ambassador of Gabon and Yoram

my stepfather when the water broke. In total panic, we rushed out and got into the nearest taxi directing him to the hospital.

I was in full labor and the driver kept begging me, *"Lady, lady, please hold on! Cross your legs and wait till we get to the hospital. This is my new cab, I can't afford to get it dirty."* When we got to the hospital Dr. Perl was not there. Because the baby was so big they knocked me out and I awoke to Dr. Perl telling me, *"It's a boy, a ten pound boy!"*

I held little Miki in my arms and looked into his eyes. A strange feeling came over me. I felt this child would somehow have a different destiny. He kept looking back at me perfectly focused.

I was very lonely at the hospital. During visiting hours, when everyone had husbands and family around them, I was alone. My mother worked and my stepfather had to look after Dani. Children were not allowed to visit. An impoverished Israeli writer came to visit me daily. Yigal Mossinsohn had married Revson's (owner of Revlon) daughter. The father promptly disowned her and they lived in a dismal apartment with their baby. Yigal had no work permit so he was moonlighting on construction sites when he could. I always have found that the poorest people in my life were the most generous and giving, both in material help, but above all, time. Yigal has been dead a long time but I shall always remember him with love and gratitude.

When I took the baby home from the hospital, Dani was terribly excited to have a new playmate. First he wanted to know where the wind up key was on the baby's back, and then notified me of a serious concern—that his new brother had no teeth.

One day my stepfather got out at the wrong exit from the subway and ran into a childhood friend from Petroseny, his hometown. One thing led to another and his friend George Hoffman, who was helping fashion businesses import European garments, introduced me to Mr. Thayer, a knitwear manufacturer. Because I could not work legally, if I got the job, Mr. Hoffman would receive my salary, and I would get it in cash from him.

I went to Macy's to buy material for a dress for the interview when the woman behind the counter fainted. She had just heard an announcement I hadn't listened to. President Kennedy had been shot.

Mr. Thayer's company occupied a whole floor in a building on Seventh Avenue. I was very nervous before the interview. My life really depended on getting this job. I was ushered into the showroom to meet him. The large showroom was decorated in dark purple with wall-to-wall antiqued mirrors. Mr. Thayer entered. He was a tall, thin middle-aged man with a brusque manner. He asked me what I thought of his showroom. I don't know what possessed me to blurt out, *"I think it looks like whorehouse."* He looked stunned and then asked me to follow him into his office. He gave me a blank check and told me to re-decorate the showroom. He then took me into the warehouse, pulled out a knitted garment, and asked me if I knew how the garment was made on a knitting machine. I had no idea, but I said I knew all about it.

I was hired as resident designer. I felt intoxicated and overjoyed. I walked to the subway looking up at the skyscrapers feeling such power! Yes, I was going to conquer New York. After all, I could do anything. I could fly!

My first job was redecorating the showroom. When going to the butcher I noticed the meat looked better than at home in the kitchen. I found out they used special lights to enhance the meat's color. I ordered all the showroom lights to be replaced with the butcher lights. I had the ceiling and woodwork painted pale beige, ordered a terra cotta color carpet, and replaced all the dark, antique mirrors with regular mirrors leaning slightly backwards. This made people seem thinner and taller. I replaced the furniture with colorful beach chairs and put a few large palm plants in the corners. When the buyers came and looked at themselves in the mirror, they looked taller, slimmer, and had nice skin color. The palm trees made them think of vacations. They felt happy, so they ordered more garments. The turnover went up dramatically. Mr. Thayer loved me. I could do no wrong. I was going to accompany him to Europe and design sample garments at the factories.

I hated working on Seventh Avenue. You were as good as your last design—not even your last collection—and the people surrounding me were a sad bunch. Finding out my husband was not with me, a lot of them offered to sleep with me to put me out of my misery. It never occurred to them to ask themselves, why would a pretty twenty-four year old woman want to sleep with a pathetic overweight fifty-plus, balding salesman?

I put them off as politely as I could. One of the lines I frequently used during my

Seventh Avenue, New York

youth was, *"As you are so attractive, I would not be able to just have an affair with you. I would fall in love and want to marry you, and your wife would find out. You don't want to go there."* Amazingly they believed me, gratefully took my advice and became my friends and protectors.

One of my pet peeves was the ubiquitous muzak. I knew which day of the week it was by the tunes they played. It was mind numbing. I had to do something. One day I stayed late after work. When the cleaners were at the other end of the floor I cut the wires in several places near the speakers. It took them weeks to repair it.

Miki was three months old when I went on my first business trip. Dani was in a pre-school and my stepfather was in charge of feeding Miki. My income was not enough to hire a nanny or even rent an apartment. I couldn't ask for more money, as this was the only job I could have with no work permit.

I met Mr. Thayer at the airport where he said, *"Goodbye, I'll see you in London."* When I found out he was flying first class and I was in economy, I told him I was going home. Either I would go first class too, or he would fly economy with me. Mr. Thayer never flew first class again.

Having grown up in Israel with no class system, I couldn't understand it. I called him Milton, explaining that even Moshe Dayan, the Israeli national hero and defense minister, was never called Mr. Dayan, just Moshe.

London was our first stop. We checked into the Dorchester Hotel, a suite with a living room and two bedrooms. I was fast asleep when I woke up to the sound of women giggling, running, and squealing in the living room. I opened my door a crack to see Milton chasing two girls around, all three of them stark naked. I quickly shut my door and went back to sleep. I must say Milton never made a pass at me and remained my friend and mentor until he died of a heart attack. I hope pursuing his favorite game, laughing, and chasing some naked girl. He was a kind man. Milton had another quirk. When checking out of the Palace Hotel in Rome, they made him open his suitcase and out came a hotel bathrobe and a coffee pot. He liked to collect stolen souvenirs.

In London we went to a firm called "Lana Knit" where I was to design some of the first samples of the coming season. It was owned and run by Frici and his older partner Mishi. I met Frici in his office. He was a very striking character at the time—around forty, charming, tanned, with a ready smile and an intense intelligence. He had had the high cheekbones and wild eyes of a Tatar. Who knows what strange mixtures of blood we middle Europeans carry.

His sister who was visiting him was in his office when I entered. "Lara," she said looking at me, "She looks like Lara". I was very flattered. The movie Dr. Zsivago just came out starring beautiful Julie Christie as Lara.

Dodi, a wonderful talented painter, kind, intelligent and loving, became my dearest friend in London and, even after I moved to America, we visited and talked on the phone a lot. When she died, I lost my very last close connection to the world that once existed. I think of her a lot, I miss her very much…Rest in peace my friend.

We stayed in London just three days. I designed and started some samples which, when ready, were going to be checked and collected by me when I was back in Europe.

We continued to Rome to visit factories and design samples, and then on to Belgium to "Bonneterie de Brabant" on the outskirts of Brussels. The owner of this company was Eddie, a Dutchman in his late thirties, tall, handsome, and

Painting by Dodi Strasser

charismatic. He lived in Brussels during the week and flew home to his family every weekend on his private plane. I had never met anyone as glamorous and charming. I was overweight after childbirth, I felt poor and dowdy. Yet there was an instant spark—no, not a spark, a fire, between us. Mr. Thayer told me, no fraternizing with suppliers, so it was just long looks between us, long looks full of promise.

Our next stop was in Milan, Italy, where we went to Alex Mann's company by the same name. Alex was a Hungarian Jew from a small town. He had escaped the Holocaust while he was in Argentina and came back to find his whole family exterminated. It was the sheer ambition born out of a poor childhood and despair that drove him to succeed. Tall, dark, and exotic-looking, he married a very wealthy older Italian countess, Cicetta, who set him up in business and coached him into high society. He dressed beautifully, had courtly manners, and enormous charm. Above all, he had exquisite taste, and his company produced wonderful knitwear. It was easy to design for his company. As I got ideas, I would sit down and sketch a garment in a few minutes and give explicit visual directions how I wanted the details to look. This impressed most people, especially Alex, who immediately offered me a job in Milan. Mr. Thayer insisted that I finish the season for him and so, with heavy heart, we went back to New York.

I was infatuated with Europe and infatuated with Eddie, who was one of the executives that we were buying merchandise from. I had met him in Belguim. When I came back to New York there was a huge long white box waiting for me. A dozen long stemmed red roses. Eddie had sent them. When I flew back to Europe on my own to check the samples Eddie flew to meet me at each airport, as I arrived. Who could resist such a courtship? Of course, his wife didn't understand him. He was going to leave her soon and I was the love of his life. These thoughts somehow legitimized the relationship in my eyes.

My stepfather who was in charge of Miki's formula accidentally doubled the concentrate and the baby looked months older, although I have been away only two weeks. My parents over sterilized everything that came in touch with the baby and strains between us started to build. I couldn't wait to get to Italy to be a grown up again. It is very hard to go home to be a child after years of independence.

The trip was wonderful. Work during the day, and dinner and nights with Eddie for ten unforgettable days. My imminent move to Italy loomed large and promising. Only a few more weeks! In New York, the roses kept coming and so did love letters, which Eddie made me promise to destroy after I read them. He would do the same with mine.

My collection was a great success and Mr. Thayer would make Alex Mann his main supplier when I went to work for him. Mann could not get a work permit for me either. It seemed Israeli passports were not welcome. Nevertheless, I was determined and when Miki was six months old I packed up my two kids and sparse belongings and left for Milan. My parents were devastated and worried. I can still hear my mother's sobs as we left, and now that I am old, I can understand the pain she must have felt. I now feel guilty. But at the time I just forged ahead to do what I wanted, no thought of the broken hearts I left behind.

VI.
MILAN

We arrived in Milan and Alex sent a car to meet us. They drove us to an apartment he rented for me that was empty except for a bed and a big cardboard box with some bedding. There was no food, no phone, no furniture of any kind and the floors were thick with dust. I made a cot for Miki out of the cardboard box and lay down on the narrow bed with Dani. *"I want to go home,"* said Dani crying. Miki started to cry too, and I cried with them. I felt desperately lonely and scared. We cried ourselves to sleep.

In the morning I got the children up and we all went out to eat something. Alex had advanced me a month's wages but I didn't speak a word of Italian. So I took a pencil and started drawing the things I needed. I got a baby carriage, cleaning supplies, food, a table, and four chairs. Luckily, I had brought formula, baby food, and diapers in my luggage. I also bought some toys to keep the children quiet and we took a taxi to the factory. The secretary ordered a phone line for me and gave me two addresses for daycare. Alex was sympathetic but busy and Cicetta, his wife, was far too glamorous and noble to help.

I thought it would be easy to find a nice motherly nanny, but women in Milan shunned housework. They preferred to work in factories. So off to the daycare we went. The first one only took babies up to two so they sent us to another one where they had older children. I left both children crying at their new daycare places, and went to a store that gave me furnishings and household goods on a monthly payment plan. I more or less set up house and picked up the boys.

I was to start work at eight in the morning, six days a week. I would get up at six and bundle up the boys. We'd hop on the first bus and take Dani to daycare. Miki and I would take another bus and drop him off. Then, I'd take another bus to work. This would be repeated every evening. It was not too bad when the weather was good, but winter soon set in and it became very difficult.

Eddie drove to see me every three weeks, but babysitting was a problem and I had very little free time. The roses and the love letters kept coming. The end came when Eddie tore up one of my letters in his car. The wind blew the pieces back through the open back window. His wife found them and pieced the letter together. Eddie's mother was dying of cancer. He told me that on her deathbed she made Eddie promise to leave me to keep the family intact. I was devastated but believed him. Now that I am older and wiser I wonder. Was it true?

Because of my prior knowledge of Romanian and French, Italian came easy to me. In three months I was fluent. Nobody spoke English at the factory so I had to learn their language. The women were wonderful to me. They babysat for me, invited me to their homes, and my children were also welcome. All Italians love children and are very generous and giving, especially the poor. I always found the less people have the more giving they are. Italian men are boys until they die. They love their mothers who spoil them and when they marry, la mamma is still the dominant force. The daughter-in-law has to continue the unconditional adoration or else. Men are fashionably dressed, own good cars, and take off their wedding rings when out with the boys. The medallion that glints through their chest hair generally says "mamma," and their long-suffering wives bring up their sons to become selfish, adored, indulged, man-children just like their fathers. By and large, as a race, Italians are good-looking and I found myself extremely popular with their beautiful young men. Whenever I found someone to babysit I went out dancing and dining and sometimes making love with a succession of beautiful boys. I suppose I was trying to recapture my carefree youth.

At work there were problems. Alex, who always prided himself in his linguistic abilities, became very jealous and resentful of my near perfect Italian. He belittled me any time I made the smallest mistake and often screamed at me. One day I had enough and left slamming the door behind me. As I ran down the stairs I half listened for him to call me back. No sound. I kept running, but much slower, eventually I was running in place very noisily. Finally the factory door opened and Alex called me back. What a relief! It was the only job I could have—especially without a work permit.

Every three months I had to leave Italy, cross into France to Nice, and reapply at the Italian consulate to extend my tourist visa for another three months, never knowing if they would grant it. If they hadn't I could not even return to Italy to pick up the children.

I started dating a very nice rich young man who invited me to lunch with his family. He suggested I bring only one child to break the ice. Divorce was not done in Italy and one did not court married women. I came with Dani and we all sat around an elegant table eating. A man with a goatee arrived and walked in. Dani looked at him and pointing to his beard, in perfect loud and clear Italian said: "My mamma has one of those but it slipped down here," pointing to his pants. Italians were pretty conservative at that time. I never saw the man again.

I started dating beautiful Gianfranco, who lived with his identical twin brother Gianpiero and his mother. She didn't have a husband and pretended to be a widow. But she did have a lover who supported them in style but did not live with them. It was all very proper and hypocritical. Gianfranco was my age but his mother was scandalized by his relationship with a woman with two kids and created merry hell. I decided to play a trick on her. I bought ten dozen eggs and had one of the boys from the factory deliver it to her. She opened the door and asked, "Where do these eggs come from?" The boy replied, "One by one from the butt of a chicken!" I would have loved to see her face.

One evening I was stood up by Gianfranco and waited at the restaurant for a long time. I knew he frequented a new restaurant nearby. Sure enough, I saw him there with a girl. The restaurant had a marble floor. I walked up to their table took the wine glass from a startled Gianfranco. With a smile dropped it on the floor next to the table. It sounded like a bomb. I left smiling. "Fare brutta figura" (losing face) was the worst thing feared by conformist Italians. It was fun!

I was an anomaly in Italy—young, married but single, self- supporting, the mother of two children, and Jewish. The women at the factory had no problem accepting me and I made some wonderful friends. I put some of them on the pill, which was new, and illegal in Italy. One of the girls was being abused by her philandering husband. He wanted her to keep having more babies and he knocked her about. I put her on the pill and talked her into hitting her sleeping husband on the head with a heavy object. She didn't kill him but he never hit her again. I imported the pill from America and felt like a crusader for women. I still feel good about it.

A young boy of sixteen used to bring us sandwiches and coffee from a local restaurant. He was always flirting with me so I told him, *"Gianni, stop it, I am older than you!"* *"Ah, Signora,"* he answered *"Vechia galina fa buona minestra!* (Old hens make good soup!)"* he said in his heavy Milanese accent.

Dani embarrassed me again. We were at a restaurant with a group of people, one of whom I was trying to impress. When a dish was put in front of him he said, *"I can't eat this. It will burn my arse hole!"*

When Miki was eleven months old he got very sick with double pneumonia and scarlet fever. He was hospitalized and I feared for his life. They had him in a small room lying on a cot with his little hands tied to the bed so he wouldn't try to climb out. The nuns were very nice and smuggled me in sometimes for a whole night to sit and watch him struggling to breathe. I used to tie myself to the chair, so I wouldn't fall off when I fell asleep. One day I arrived and his cot was empty! After hearing my screams they took me to a ward where they moved him to because he was no longer contagious. After they calmed me down, a young doctor came to talk to me and said, "Signora, the boy should be fine, but, anyway, you are so young, you will have many more children." I came close to slapping the idiot! No wonder Italian medical schools were the easiest to graduate from! Lots of people who couldn't get into schools in the United States or Europe went to Italy to study medicine. God help their patients!

Miki stayed in a convalescent hospital for two months and I was told he would not thrive in the polluted air of Milan. He was getting sick more often since we moved to Milan I had to find a solution.

One of the men at work was from the hills, about an hour from Milan and offered to have Miki stay with his wife and mother. A family nearby wanted to take care of Dani as well. With a heavy heart I took the boys to a village called Pontremoli in the Tuscan hills and left them there. I would visit every Sunday. Soon Dani spoke fluent Italian. Miki slept in a big bed between the grandma "La Nonna" and the wife. He loved it. Michele, as they called him, started getting pink cheeks because of the fresh air. They were both thriving.

The people in the village decided to save the children and baptize them in the local church in the village of Pontremoli. I only found out later when I saw a picture of Dani being baptized. There was no photograph of Miki during this event. When I found the picture I thanked the people. What harm can a ceremony do? After all, they did it with such love and concern.

My work was going very well. My designs were successful and Alex Mann, my boss, had exquisite taste. I learned a lot. One afternoon, as I was leaving work he asked me to deliver a dress to a lady who was staying at a very posh hotel in Milan. The dress was to be a present for her nineteen- year old daughter. I arrived at the hotel and took the parcel up to her room. The imperious Hungarian woman looked at the dress and handed it back to me saying her daughter would not wear anything as common as that. I was stunned by her rudeness. After all, the dress was a gift. As I was leaving she handed me a tip. I debated whether I should throw it back into her face, but it was not a small sum. I thanked her and took it. I cried all the way home. I felt cheap and humiliated.

Dani's baptism

It was during this time that I became addicted to Opera. I went to La Scala at every opportunity and could only afford the standing places at the very top. I stood happily. The acoustics were such that I heard every note. Among other great performances I saw Maria Callas singing Tosca. It was a magical and unforgettable event!

I sent Yoram a ticket to come

La Scala in Milan

and visit the boys. When he arrived we couldn't find a ride to go to Pontremoli. Yoram said, "Don't worry I haven't seen Miki since he was born. I am sure one more day won't make a difference." I knew then that I had to put a final end to the marriage. He was still my great love and best friend, but no longer my husband.

Alex and George Hoffman (who got me my job in America) decided to send me to Lisbon, Portugal where they were planning to open a factory because labor there was very cheap. They sent me to talk to a man who would possibly invest in the venture. I now realize I was sent as bait.

I was met in Lisbon by George Spitzer, a scruffy, homely, sixty-year-old man. He took me stay with him and his mother in an exquisite antique villa on a hill overlooking the whole city. The house and garden were surrounded by a high wall that was accessed by a huge carved door. Priceless Aubusson wall hangings lined the hall and the house was furnished with beautiful antique pieces. It was like a museum! Mr. Spitzer's formidable mother who was in her eighties met me at the top of the stairs, looming like a huge fat evil queen.

She decided that I should marry her son and tied to talk me into it. I made polite excuses saying that I was still married, and anyway I had two little children. She calmly replied, "Oh, there are great boarding schools for children of any age." George Spitzer was old, smelly, and had tufts of stringy graying hair. I was twenty-five and not interested. They were incredibly rich and terminally stingy. After dinner Mrs. Spitzer took two apples to the kitchen to be shared by the three house servants. I was curious how she could divide just two apples among three people? "It is very simple my dear," she explained. "You cut each apple into three parts."

George and his mother shared a bedroom—which was pretty strange in itself—but they were abnormally close and protective of each other. George apparently made his money salvaging ships during the war, and was banned from entering most European countries except France. They also had an antique Rolls Royce I think a Silver Shadow, but didn't use it much because it was too extravagant on gas. He used a small decrepit car to get around in. I would have rather starved than become part of this family.

One night I went out alone to have dinner with a friend who happened to be visiting from New York. I asked for the front door key so I wouldn't disturb the house later when I was coming back. The key was twelve inches long!

Mrs. Spitzer was most persistent. She kept telling me that they wanted someone to inherit their fortune—that she was eighty-eight and George would need a wife to care for him. To tempt me even further George Spitzer asked me to detour through Paris when flying back to Milan because he wanted me to see his Parisian house. I agreed because I wanted to go to my beloved Paris again. I also knew it would please Alex if I showed a little polite interest in their potential investor.

In Paris, I gave the taxi the address and we arrived at a gate blocking the street guarded by two very fancy gendarmes. This was the gate to the small very exclusive enclave of a few houses that included the French president's official residence. I got saluted every time I passed through that gate! This was also a magnificently furnished baroque townhouse with a butler in attendance, but I couldn't wait to leave. Needless to say, the Spitzers never invested in the new factory. After my return to Milan, Spitzer sent me a box of orchids, but being so stingy, he sent it surface mail. The orchids arrived like limp lettuce. I wonder if mother and son were buried with their wealth.

When I got back to Milan I was offered the job of running the new knitwear factory in Portugal. My Italian salary would make me better off in Lisbon, and I could have the children in a much healthier environment. I accepted the job immediately and had exactly three days to pack up the kids and anything we wanted take on the plane with us. Everything else I either sold or gave away. I said tearful goodbyes to all the people who helped me so much. When I drove off with Miki, Nonna, the ancient toothless grandma, ran after the car with tears streaming down her face calling, "Ciao, Michele, ciao caro mio!"

VII.
LISBON

In Lisbon I found a nice furnished apartment in a very good neighborhood. It had three bedrooms, a living room, and elegant dining room. I hired a kindly middle-aged woman to be nanny to the boys. Her name was Maria de Lourdes. It seemed that every woman had Maria added to her name.

I hired a maid-cook called Maria Elena and lived like a queen for a while. I would come home from the factory and be served an excellent dinner with starched napkins and great wine. Even my bed linen was starched and ironed. A car came for me every day to take me to work. Other than the blatantly visible social ills of the society I found myself in, I was very comfortable.

At the time, Portugal was under the dictatorship of Salazar and it was very much a country of two classes—the rich and the poor. The rich were very rich, and the poor seemed to be poorer than anywhere I'd seen before. Portugal was also incredibly religious and had very strict moral rules, which, of course, applied more to the poor than the rich. The concept of a young woman with children, without a man, if not a widow dressed in black, was very suspect. The lace curtains of my watchful neighbors would flick whenever I set foot outside.

The factory was housed outside the city in a poor area. The workers were mainly from this area, and they were paid one dollar a day. My bosses didn't realize that if you pay someone a dollar a day, you only get a dollar's worth of work. The workers in the factory were so poor, they would have to leave their children in the courtyard while they worked, and there was no shade or shelter. I hired a nanny for the children, put up an open tent, and got some toys and swings. I also made sure they were fed a decent lunch and a snack.

I was also instructed to fire anyone I suspected of being pregnant because the factory was responsible for paid maternity leave. Of course I couldn't do this and got into lots of trouble with my bosses. One day one of the mothers brought me a present, a carefully wrapped egg from one of her hens. The gift touched me more than any other present I ever received. This woman was so poor that this egg was more precious to her than an expensive store bought item. I felt very honored and at the same time very ashamed of my comparatively luxurious life.

The boys were getting used to Lourdes but had problems communicating with her because of the language. I enrolled Dani in a posh English school, which I could barely afford. George Hoffman, who became a partner in the factory, moved to Lisbon with his wife and two daughters. When I ran into his wife at the school she looked down her nose and said, "I can't believe your child is at this school! We must be paying you too much."

Frici came over from London to visit the Hoffmans, and asked them to invite me to dinner. Mrs. Hoffman refused, saying she didn't believe in socializing with hired staff. Hearing this Frici packed his case, moved to a beautiful hotel, and invited me over. I spent the night in his arms sobbing my heart out. Crying for the humiliations, for the life I missed in Israel where I was somebody, for my marriage, for Yoram whom I missed so, for my fatherless boys, for my insecure future, for the unfamiliar world I lived in, for my old friends, for my

School uniforms

past, and for the fear of the future. Frici was wonderful to me. He just held me and let me cry for hours and hours. I started feeling like I used to in my father's arms, loved, secure, and safe—until he flew back to London.

One of my jobs was to deal with customs at the port where the yarn from Italy was delivered. After dealing with the petty bureaucracy of customs, they weighed the merchandise on board the ship before releasing it. No one realized that the yarn absorbed moisture during the sea voyage, and weighed more than what the documentation stated. Hours, after all this was sorted out, finally, they agreed to let us have the yarn. In the meantime, they unloaded a shipment of live cattle and the dock was covered in excrement from the poor stressed animals. The crane with the nets of wool yarn swung over the dock for unloading into a waiting truck. At this point, the net broke and the parcels of open yarn tumbled onto the dockside covered in manure!

Other problems kept slowing down production. The knitting machines kept breaking down and the largely unskilled labor had no clue how to fix the problems. We had one mechanic from Italy, but he was an alcoholic who was out of it most of the time. We kept missing delivery dates and the cash dried up. My bosses decided to close the factory and we were all out of a job.

We had to move out of the apartment. Luckily a friend I made in Lisbon had a small rather derelict beach cottage in a seaside town nearby and the children and I moved in. The nanny and the cook came with us because they had nowhere else to go, and so I was in the ridiculous position of being the mistress of a well run shack. I started writing to Yoram for help but he had no money to send me. My parents helped with what they could but they had very little too. My old boss from New York heard of my plight and sent me a present, one thousand dollars! To me it was a fortune. He saved my life.

I finally got a job doing a television program in Lisbon. I was to talk about fashion and sketch. For my first appearance the whole village congregated in the local café that had a TV set. It was a big deal to have a celebrity in town.

The studio was in a huge warehouse with a leaky roof. After being made up like a tart, I was ushered in, told to stand in a chalk circle, and the cameras were turned on. I introduced myself and started sketching on a big easel. It was fine until it started to rain on me, dissolving the thick make-up, which started running down my face. So I stepped out of the circle to find a dry spot. The cameraman motioned to me angrily to get back into the circle when I suddenly said, "Don't be stupid, can't you see it's raining?" Not only was I rude, but my Portuguese was very poor. I had only been in the country for five months. All I knew I picked up at the factory. The next morning the papers panned me. One paper said, "If we are to hire rude people, at least hire someone who can speak Portuguese!" So I was unemployed again.

Felipe de Sousa

At the TV station I met a man who was the music director of the station. He was forty-two and looked older, heavy set with a swarthy complexion, and receding curly hair. I was twenty-six and looked like his daughter. He fell in love with me and courted me in a very sweet old-fashioned way. Felipe de Sousa would bring me flowers and take me to wonderful restaurants. He never touched me and treated me with courtly respect. He used the respectful "thou" instead of "you." He even wrote a symphony dedicated to me. It is a pretty boring symphony, but, hey! How many people can say someone wrote a symphony for them? Felipe came from a very wealthy family and was divorced. He asked me to marry him. No, I did not love him, but my children needed to live somewhere decent and there was no way I could find a job. I told him I would think about it. He invited me to meet his mother and aunt. They all lived in a beautiful Villa that had a sweeping staircase into a large hall, which also housed the music room. When I arrived at dinner the two women were dressed in black and their hostile disapproval was palpable. After all, here I was, a Jew with two kids and no husband, obviously after their good Catholic son—being young and pretty spelled trouble. There was also an uncle who came in for a few minutes to look me over. They all loathed me. I felt angry and humiliated, and decided to hit back. I started talking about my family, about a maternal great aunt who married a circus midget in Budapest and talked about my mother's sister who was a dancer and whore in Tangier. If they were going to hate me I wanted to give them good reason. After dinner, poor scandalized Felipe drove me home and explained that he was going to marry me no matter what. He also told me about his ex-wife.

With Dani and Miki in Portugal

Felipe was studying music in

Vienna. In fact, one of his fellow students was Zubin Mehta, who was poor and starving. Felipe didn't think he would amount to much. It is here that he met a vivacious German girl who became his wife. He brought her home to the family villa. Every Friday night, old musicians would play the most obscure Portuguese baroque pieces for hours while mother and aunt sat dressed in black, crocheting. The poor young wife finally lost it and rebelled. During a concert she walked down the sweeping staircase stark naked! I sympathize with the poor girl. She then ran away and Felipe hired a detective to find her. The detective ended up marrying her.

I was rather worried about becoming Felipe's wife for reasons other than the great difference in age and culture. I was still young and liked to joke around. I liked to dance to sing and play silly games with the kids. I wasn't ready to become a nineteenth-century matron.

I found an old bicycle in the cottage and rode around town on it. I was riding on a deserted road when Felipe's uncle tried to run me over. He came within inches of my rear wheel when I managed to drive into a ditch to escape. He sped off and denied ever having been in the area. I felt my life would always be in danger if I married Felipe.

I was still not divorced from Yoram. I was hoping something would come up, a job somewhere.

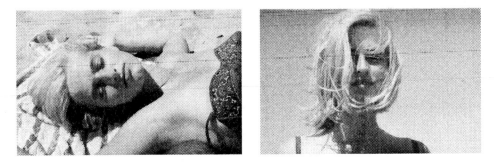

On the beach In Portugal

VIII.
LONDON

Frici and his business partner Mishi at *"Lana Knit"* invited me to London on a two-week trial—to work and see if I was suitable and needed there. I left the boys in the care of the nanny and flew to London full of hope. During my two weeks, I excelled and they decided to start organizing a work permit for my employment. I was overjoyed. As I was ready to fly back to Lisbon I got a call from Lourdes (the nanny) who told me Miki was paralyzed and couldn't walk. As I arrived at the shack, Miki came running to greet me! The paralysis disappeared. The guilt never did. I was always working and my poor boys were being raised by surrogates, without a proper home, without a father.

I broke up gently with Felipe. I would have probably made him very unhappy, and he was a kind man who didn't deserve it. I found out later that when there was a revolution in Mozambique where he was born, he went back there to help build a new utopia. I believe he was killed by the opposition. Those were turbulent times. I have never been able to trace him.

I left the children with Lourdes and went back to London to start work, find an apartment, and get ready to bring the children to their new home. In London, it was almost impossible to find an apartment that would allow children. The British have a great love for pets but not for children. They are tolerated at best. After all, what other language refers to a young child as an *"it?"* I saw apartment after apartment. Whenever I mentioned the children I was turned away. One in particular got me very angry. It was dirty, with cigarette burns on the furniture and on the nasty blue carpet. The snooty landlady shook her head at the mere mention of children. I screamed at her, "I would not want my children to live in this squalid dump unfit for animals. Keep your filthy flat!" I stormed out slamming the door after me. It felt good. I finally found a two bedroom, small, unfurnished apartment opposite a church in Belsize Park, got a loan from Mishi and bought enough beds and dishes to bring the children over.

We arrived at Heathrow Airport in the evening, but we were singled out and made to wait in a separate area. We waited and waited and waited. Three nasty immigration officials interrogated me for hours. First, they accused me of not looking like a fashion designer. Then, after asking me how many languages I spoke, they accused me of being a spy. Apparently there was some discrepancy with my work permit and they threatened to put me on the next plane to Israel. It was past midnight when they finally released us, after seven hours of not allowing the children, who were aged six and two, a drink or a snack. An acquaintance, a young man, was waiting for us for hours. He too had been questioned and asked if he was intending to pimp for me in London? These men were horrible, the typical small-minded nothings who, when given a little power and authority, take it upon themselves to persecute anyone they can. They visibly enjoyed toying with the children and me.

Finally, we were at home in the little flat and I started to decorate it as fast as my salary would allow. I enrolled Dani in a nearby school. Nanny Lourdes was at home with little Miki. As Mishi lived close to my flat, I was able to commute to work with him. I loved the old man very much. He was wise, funny, and incredibly malicious if he disliked someone. He had a wicked sense of humor and could destroy someone with a quick funny remark. He had a friend who married a woman thirty-five years younger than him. At a party, Mishi introduced them as "Joseph and his widow to be." Mishi, with his kind wife Flora, sort of adopted me, and I spent many evenings at their house, feeling loved and being advised with great wisdom.

I felt very alone and didn't know anyone in London. I also fell desperately and hopelessly in love with Frici. He was everything a man should be—intelligent, charming, talented, creative, successful, decisive, and exuded power and self confidence. He looked a lot like Nureyev, the ballet dancer, in his early days. There was a wild, windswept look about him, high cheekbones and wild bright eyes. When he entered a room he dominated it without saying a word. He was married to a beautiful English woman and had three lovely daughters. At this point in his life he wanted to forget his past. He and his sister were born in Yugoslavia. In an area home to many Hungarians, their mother tongue was, in fact, Hungarian. Their father was a prominent lawyer who died just before the war, and both he and his sister were in Budapest when the Nazis deported their mother. She perished. Dodi survived in a house protected by the Swedish Consulate, and Frici was friends with a cabinet minister's son. He passed himself off as a Christian and lived in constant terror of being found out and killed. At night, when everyone slept, he would creep down to the cellar and create false identity documents for Jews in hiding. I found out snippets of this from other people. He never felt heroic about all the people he saved.

When Frici arrived in England, he—as many others of his generation—decided to put an end to their former, unbearably sad lives and start anew. Forget Judaism. Marry and raise new families, in a new, painless world. Their children went to church, were educated as English children, and were never told much about the painful past of their Jewish parents. They became rich, and did their best to be accepted in English upper class society. "It's all about getting your children into the right school," I was told repeatedly.

I started meeting people and going out, with several more or less suitable young men, but people don't pursue women with two children. Frici had very little time and we saw each other very little other than at work. For me, he was my rock, my only security, the only person I was trying to impress, but he did not belong to me. He had a whole other established life with the mother of his children. I was obviously closer to him intellectually due to a common background. I gave him books such as André Schwartz-Bart's *"The Last of the Just"* and books by Eli Wiesel to somehow break this carapace, of his near denial. I felt that he needed to reconnect with his Jewish soul to be whole again. I take credit for having achieved this, though it must be harder to live with the burdens of the past. I think that ultimately it made him a much kinder and better person.

Dear Frici,

As you lie in your hospital bed, drifting in and out of consciousness, can you feel my love and my sorrow? I know you want to die, but I find it very hard to imagine a world without you. You are the rock, the pillar, and the very core of so many of us. I cannot believe I won't be able to pick up the phone to hear your voice, ask for your advice, and hear your encouraging words. Minds such as yours should not be allowed to die. Great men such as you should not die. You are far too valuable and necessary for all of us who came into your orbit.

I have known and loved you for forty-four years. I remember when I first set eyes on you in "Lana Knit," the knitting factory you had in the east end of London. I was brought there by my American boss to design some samples for New York. I was twenty-four and had just had a baby two months before. I felt fat and ugly but you walked in and filled the room with your incredible charisma and strength. The first impression I had was that there was wildness in your face. I thought of the Mongolian steppes, a wild conqueror riding a wild stallion. I wanted to be near you. I wanted to bask in your light. I wanted to stay.

I had to go back to New York and didn't see you until we met again in Portugal. You asked my boss to invite me to lunch with you but his snob of a wife informed you that she did not like to associate with the "hired help." So you left their house and spent the whole weekend with me. It came so naturally. I remember lying in your arms sobbing for a long time, for losing my roots yet again, for all the hardships I had, for the father I never had and the cosmic loneliness I felt so often. I felt so secure in your arms but I knew you had a life of your own—a wife and children—and that the next day you would be gone. There was such an emotional connection between us. We talked and talked and talked and I cried some more.

A year passed before I saw you again. You and your partner, Mishi, hired me to work for your new company Nova Knit. Of course, it was impossible for you to see me much. But I lived for those few stolen hours. Do you remember that beautiful weekend in Cap D'Antibes when you taught me to drive your boat, Alcariv, and you parasailed behind? I turned and looked at you high up in the sky, laughing, happy, wild, the wind blowing your hair. We were so happy, so young. I went up to the room to rest and you met a woman downstairs who had seen you with your family. She said only one thing. "Be careful. You can always spot the children of divorce no matter how old they are when it happens." You came up and told me and I agreed but it was so hard. I fantasized living with you but I knew it would never happen.

I felt that you lacked roots and that you tried to put the past behind you. So I started to influence you to embrace being a Jew. Not as a religion, but to accept the inevitability of a collective connection. I gave you books. You read voraciously. You made several trips to Israel and found a sort of peace within your soul. I am so proud of having been able to give you this gift of identity. For better or worse, you belonged much more.

Mishi advised me to make a life for myself separate from you. After all, you didn't want to get divorced and lose your children. Mishi rightly said, "You cannot build a house on ruins." So I went out with people, and eventually got married, had a successful career, and made a lot of money. But I never got to share my life with you, my great love.

I wish I had the chance to spend years with you, to nurture and love you, and, above all, unite our souls more than we had the chance. We would have been good together, good for one another. I would have looked after you, kept you calm and whole. Now you are leaving me, my best friend. I thank you for giving me some of yourself, for loving me, encouraging me, for believing in my talent, and my intellect. I thank you for calling me a lot during my cancer treatments and for coming to visit me when I had my car accident. I thank you for always being there. Above all, I thank you for just being. Goodnight, my love, my friend.

A photo I took of Frici
in the south of France

Frici had always been an advocate of being able to control one's last days. He was a member of several organizations, such as the Hemlock Society. Unfortunately, his wish has not come to pass. He was ill and was transported to a hospital in London where he died in September of 2008.

I started seeing a young theatrical agent, Al Mitchell, a cockney. People were scandalized by his accent and I couldn't understand why. I was also seeing a really nice, very intelligent man, a lawyer. We used to go dancing for hours and hours but somehow there was not enough chemistry. I was still very lonely. My soul was lonely. I was so tired.

I had finished furnishing my apartment and hung up the last mirror. When Mishi and Frici with their families were all away on holiday in France I had, what must have been, a total mental breakdown. Very efficiently, I arranged airline tickets for Lourdes to go back to Portugal and for the boys to go back to Israel to their father. I left all my belongings to charity, left instructions for my cremation, and wrote letters to my parents and my boys. I didn't think anyone else cared. I sent Lourdes and the boys to stay with a friend in the country for the weekend and locked myself in the apartment. I drank a bottle of Gin and swallowed a whole bottle of sleeping pills. For good measure, I also tried to cut my wrists but I just bled profusely, without fatal harm. I was semi-conscious, stumbling around leaning against the bloody wall when I tripped over a small toy, a dalek. Suddenly I realized what I was doing to my children. How could I leave them orphaned, being swept like corks on the sea, without a mother? How could I be so cold and heartless to hurt them so? I imagined their little faces crying in despair, and as I was about to pass out, I made a last desperate effort to live. The only number I remembered was

Al Mitchell's, who miraculously happened to be home with the flu. Apparently, I was not able to finish telling him what happened before I fell unconscious. He called the police, who somehow opened the door and took me to the nearest hospital. I came to, as they were pumping my stomach, screaming at me to stay awake. Up to a week before it was a crime to commit suicide in England, and if you survived, there was a prison sentence waiting to cheer you up.

The only available bed was in the cancer ward where I found myself surrounded by women desperate to live. Miraculously, they didn't hate me. They were mostly sad and baffled to see someone so young and healthy giving up on life, the very thing they were so desperately trying to hang onto. Those who could walk came and sat on my bed and told me about their battles to stay alive, their tragic illnesses, and the suffering they endured. I cried with shame and sadness, for them, for myself, and for the emptiness I still felt. My lawyer friend sent me a huge bouquet of red roses with a card that said, "Please live."

The next day they released me from the hospital. I had no coat, no handbag, no purse, and no money. I hailed a cab and told him the whole story. He took me home and made sure I found the key I always hid under the mat so could get into the apartment. He would not accept any money from me just gave me a hug and wished me a long life. I have never lost my faith in the kindness of strangers. Help always came from totally unexpected sources.

I tried to get my life together again. The hospital insisted that I see a psychiatrist so I did. He was a round, pink, very upper class Englishman. It would have taken me lifetime to connect with him, to explain my past, let alone my fears and nightmares that still to this day haunt me. So I lied, and he told me I was all better and didn't need to come back. The silly little man seemed relieved and so was I. I didn't tell Lourdes or the children but my bosses found out. They both decided to bring Yoram over to England to watch over me. He was still my closest friend. I figured I could save a lot of money if he could replace the nanny and I was also hoping he would get to know his boys.

I was going to try to see if things worked between us. Yoram didn't want to let Lourdes go. He said he needed time to write. However, he mainly sat and watched television. I would find him in the same chair when I got home from work. I was having a hard time living on my income and one day I found him outside the house taking an expensive driving lesson. Bear in mind we didn't even own a car at the time. That was it. I wanted no more marriage. No more trying. No more.

Mishi had a studio apartment in a house he bought. I rented it for Yoram. He seemed happy. He had a whisky with Mishi a few times a week and made friends easily. Young girls especially adored him. He would be sitting in a pub surrounded by adoring fans. He was a great raconteur and a brilliant cook. He never lacked invitations to talk, cook and dine. Whenever I visited Mishi and Flora, I would pop over to Yoram, pretend to use his bathroom and leave money in his medicine cabinet. We never talked about it. I didn't have much, but he had nothing and he was still my dearest friend. He was, after all, the love of my life, my mentor, my teacher, and my soul mate. Once you loved someone you can't "unlove" them. You just love them differently.

Michael Phillips

We decided to officially divorce. In Israel we could only have a religious wedding so we needed to get a religious divorce; they call it a *"get."* We went to the rabbinical court. There were four little orthodox men in full regalia sitting behind a long table. Their dangling little legs did not reach the floor. Yoram and I sat on two chairs opposite one another. They wanted to know if we were getting divorced for sex reasons, about our sex life or the lack of it, and they questioned us in a very prurient nasty way. Finally, they gave us the necessary document and off we went. We had lunch in a Greek restaurant, polished off a bottle of wine, got pretty tipsy, and went home singing in the street. It was a very happy, giggly divorce.

I went to a party where I met Michael. He was thirty-three and Jewish. He owned a fashion business with his mother and was rather distant and somewhat absent, difficult to connect with. Soon after we started going out things were getting serious. I felt comfortable with him. He was kind, liked my children, and I craved a normal secure home life.

At work I asked one of the salesman who sold me linings if he knew the firm *"Laura Phillips"* and especially Michael Phillips? *"Sure, they buy from me sometimes. I know the son too. Why do you want to know about them?"* *"Because I am getting married to Michael."* The poor man was speechless.

Michael was slow asking me to marry him so I started sending myself twelve red roses once a week. The flowers came with no card. I swore I had no idea who sent them and after the third week Michael proposed. "Will you marry me in June?" he said. I replied, "What's wrong with March?" Mother sent me a hot pink dress and coat with a matching hat and we got married in a reform synagogue. It was a strange wedding. Someone forgot the music and apparently I marched down the aisle very purposefully. I was given away by Frici's brother-in-law and the

Michael, Dani,
myself, Miki at
wedding

reception was at Michael's sisters' elegant flat. Frici's wife remarked that Miki, who was not yet three, should be in bed and discussed some brand of washing machine that was extravagant on water. The whole wedding seems to be a blur. I had the feeling I was watching it all from outside, detached, as if it was not my life at all. It was somehow a parallel reality. I smiled a lot and was kissed by lots of Jewish people—all cousins and relatives of Michael. More than ever I kept thinking of my Jewish family who were no longer. This wasn't really my life, my wedding, or my reality.

We flew to Klosters in Switzerland. Our room overlooked huge beautiful mountains. The next day, I went to ski school but abandoned it after going down the slope backwards. I was terrified and never tried skiing again. I spent the rest of the week sleeping and throwing up. I discovered I was pregnant. I rang my lawyer friend, Bernard, to tell him I married Michael, and to say goodbye. All he said was, "When you want a good divorce lawyer, call me." I was rather shocked.

Back in London we bought the lease on a house in a very unusual little enclave of five houses clustered around a small garden. The passageway had parking on the side but the central garden was pedestrian. I thought it would be great for the boys until I realized how much the neighbors disliked children. One lady used to bring a horse for visits, but kids were not welcome. There was a strange assortment of neighbors. There was Miss Wilberforce (a great-granddaughter of the famous British abolitionist) who had the visits from the horse. Then there was Elic Howe who was head of the occult misinformation fed to Hitler in World War II. Hitler believed in the occult and its signs and predictions. Elic Howe later wrote a book about it called "Urania's Children." How he managed to write the world's most boring book about such a fascinating subject is truly incomprehensible. Then there was the middle-aged man who did something in the city. He left every morning in his pin striped suit and bowler hat carrying an umbrella. In the evenings he and his wife would get tipsy and chase each other around the flowerbeds clad in their underwear. But little boys were frowned upon.

I was still working for Frici and Mishi and I had to drive to the East End of London every day. My belly got so big they had to put extensions on the pedals so I could reach them. I started noticing Michael was going out more and more. I was too tired to join him. He was also eyeing me critically, not thrilled with my new body. I think this was the period when our marriage started to unravel. As I was heavily pregnant, I got exhausted coming home at night, and I was hoping I didn't have to work to the very last day of my pregnancy. Michael made it very clear that by having married me with two children he expected me to pull my weight. He told me I was dragging myself around.

Yoram was back in Israel at this time. The premiere of the revival of his anti-war play fell on the day before the start of the Six-Day War. He also fell off the stage and broke his arm during dress rehearsal. Talk about bad luck. Due to some clerical mix up, I got call up papers from the Israeli army. I phoned Michael in his office. He immediately snapped into action and called up his uncle who was a doctor and got tranquilizers, for himself. Of course, the army realized that calling up pregnant fashion designers was no way to win a war and sent me a letter of apology.

My gynecologist Dr. Suchet was the father of David Suchet of Monsieur Poirot fame. Dr Suchet was a sweet old man and I was to be his last delivery before his retirement. I was in Holloway Hospital near the women's prison. It was dismal place but I had a private room. I was in heavy labor for hours. My mother-in-law came to see me and brought samples of linoleum for her bathroom, which she wanted to discuss. I was floating in and out of pain and longed for a woman to share it with me, to stroke my forehead and love me. I felt lonely. In those days men were still pretty much excluded from childbirth so I was alone. Eventually, I was given some drugs that knocked me out and woke up when they handed me a beautiful baby boy. Each time I gave birth I felt a huge surge of pride and defiance. Hitler missed killing me and here I am giving birth to a Jewish child! The song from *"Fiddler on the Roof"* kept playing in my head, *"To Life, to Life, Lechaim, Lechaim, Lechaim to Life!"*

Without asking me, Michael's family was going to name the baby Paul or Philip after Michael's father who died a few years earlier. I vetoed it and insisted on calling him Jonathan. When the boys were brought in to visit me little Miki took one look at his brother and whispered in my ear. "Mummy, you have a Chinese baby." Sure enough the baby was slowly turning yellow. He had jaundice.

When I went home, I decided to leave my job and work for the family business. The company was in a bankrupt situation. The family didn't want me to lose my salary. They knew nothing about my abilities. So they were very much against me coming on board. I prevailed and started working, leaving the baby with various au-pair girls.

The firm *"Laura Phillips"* was named after my mother in law. It manufactured and wholesaled cocktail dresses, but mainly dresses and coat outfits for the mother of the bride. As women of all ages were dressing younger and less formally, it was a shrinking market. Laura was over sixty and her innovative powers were in decline. We worked in completely separate ways with

In my fashion studio in London

different taste and different materials. Michael's older sister Honey was in the showroom and every time they needed to reorder cloth there would be a family meeting to discuss it. I had designed a dress and after we sold a hundred, I reordered enough cloth to make two hundred more. I didn't consult the family and all hell broke loose. Honey resigned in a huff and we ended up selling close to six hundred more of the dress.

In the morning, we would come to work and Michael would throw the key to a young salesman who would park the car at a nearby garage. Everyone clocked in, except of course the bosses. There was a lot of absenteeism. Although we only had twenty employees (the garments were manufactured by mainly Greek outdoor workers in small factories), the attendance was bad. I started by removing the clock with the time cards and when Michael panicked as to how we would check attendance, I explained, "You and I will be first in and last out. You will also park your own car as you are not a cripple!" We never again had a problem with attendance. The family resented me and it showed in many ways. When I complained that Michael who had lots of clothes tended to wear a suit until it was all wrinkled, Laura gave me a lecture about how I should lay out his clothes at night. I asked if his two sisters who didn't work did this. They didn't, but that was different. I wanted a new warm family, but they never accepted me. Once after dinner I served desert before clearing all the dishes. My mother-in-law gave me the "in this country" lecture—this one was about not serving desert before removing the dishes. I felt angry and explained that it was difficult for me to know this because where I grew up we all ate out of one big dish sitting on the floor. She didn't bat an eye at this. She must have believed it. The two older sisters were constantly criticizing every design, but it did not stop them filling their wardrobe with my dresses. The fact that I grew up in Transylvania was the source of great hilarity. I was told I have "no social aplomb" because I insisted that at a dinner a person would converse differently with a bishop or a gynecologist. Of course, it didn't help that I was younger, prettier, and more talented. They knew I loved Opera but never once invited me to join them there. I felt like Cinderella.

MY CAREER IN FASHION IN LONDON

I took over without meaning to. Although Laura was still working on her designs, I was experimenting with new things. At first, the buyers from the stores who were used to a certain type of merchandise from us balked at my designs. I remember some of them actually laughing at some dresses in the show room, while I

Kati's showroom

hid and cried behind a curtain. Somehow I prevailed, and soon we were making so much money that the accountant had to figure out new ways to save on corporate taxes. My label was "KATI" at "Laura Phillips" and I made evening and formal dresses, during a time long dresses were all the rage. I had calmed down from my early designing days and became a bit less innovative and more saleable. The showroom, which had been dull and pseudo-elegant, had to be changed. Much to

Drawing on showroom wall

everyone's chagrin I painted everything white and put down a grass green carpet. I put fresh flowers on the windowsills and changed the crystal chandeliers to spot lights. Each season I sketched life sized drawings of dresses from the new collections on the white walls and made the whole place look younger. I even retired the slippered, shuffling, rude tea lady, and hired nice smiling people to serve tea or coffee. I loved writing orders and adding them up after the buyers were gone to see how we were doing. We were doing better, and better, and better.

I started getting a lot of attention from the press. Almost every week they had stories, sketches, and photographs of my dresses and me. I became well known. Being famous in the fashion world in London was a very big achievement and I basked in the light of it. I was very proud of it, but there was also a lot of pressure. I had to be good every season and not only produce garments that were newsworthy but also provide the bread and butter styles that were the basis of our success.

I flew to New York twice a year to buy fabrics that were different from what we could find in Europe. I would order thousands of yards of fabrics I felt would look good in dresses that I would design when I got back to London. This was usually six months before the actual season, so I only had my gut level instincts to guide me. We would gamble thousands of pounds on my hunches. Sometimes I would wake up in cold sweat at night. What if I was wrong? What if I didn't guess right? What if I got the wrong colors?

Luckily, I was usually spot on. We were manufacturing and selling about two thousand garments a week. I invented a "one size fits all" dress that we manufactured thousands of. I used every kind of fabric I could think of. We even sold the dresses to cruise lines for their onboard shops. I made trouser suits, eveningwear, and even designed fabrics. I made tie-dye chiffon evening dresses in lovely shimmering pastels. I even designed some panel prints, also in lovely flowing materials. I seemed to get everything just right. The mistake I made was copying an antique sampler I had, on beige linen and made several styles of it. I changed the date on the fabric to 1972, the year I made the dresses. It looked great, but as I dated the garments they only sold for that season! Oh hubris! I didn't make that mistake twice. I copied designs from Persian carpets onto shiny knitted jersey fabrics and dyed strips of macramé lace in bright primary colors. I used several

different colored laces to trim back voile dresses. They were very pretty and very different. I used voile prints trimmed with quilted cotton of the same pattern and made several styles like that. I used to do groups of garments from the same fabrics, which also helped the fashion journalists when they did stories on "KATI" dresses. Yet somehow all this success didn't make me happy.

Dated sampler made into garment

Original fabric design   Sketches from work book

Sketches from work book

We had plenty of money, but I was working six or seven days a week and was always exhausted. After work, I would rush home to help look after the boys, who were well cared for by a succession of wonderful Filipina girls.

We were making more and more money, and I was getting unhappier and unhappier. Michael was ever more distant and ogled our seasonal model girls even more obviously. I tried to compensate by becoming extravagant. I would fly to Paris to buy wallpaper, bought new cars and had them delivered without even finding out the price, bought a holiday villa in Portugal, but I still worked long hours because I was the only one in the business who could hold it all together. Laura was getting older and Michael had no patience with humdrum work. He was swanning around, who knows where, during working hours.

I was working too hard, but the boys had everything they wanted. Dani was in a progressive vegetarian boarding school. He was very happy there and had a thriving little business of grilling pork sausages in the woods after bedtime and selling them to the students.

I should have been happy but my marriage was not working. I kept getting all kinds of minor illnesses, from kidney infections to psoriasis. I am sure they were all the result of stress. The final straw was when the husband of one of our model girls called me at home, and asked me to intervene. My husband was harassing his wife in the dressing rooms. I had a big fight with Michael and threatened to leave

My Morgan car

My horse

My house in Portugal

him. I told him I will find someone else but he brushed it off with a joke. He really did not take it seriously. I went to see his mother to try and get her to intervene. She told me, "Men do wander when they are married. You should dress more provocatively and look more attractive. After all, you have no choice now that you have three children. Just grin and bear it, like we all have done." I responded, "Laura, I got married with two children. I can find a husband with three as well."

Vacation with boys

THE ANGEL IN THE MARBLE

I met Brian Walden at a cocktail party. He was a very charismatic brilliant politician, a member of parliament, and on his way to possibly becoming prime minister. He was not handsome, but rather small and thin, nondescript, but the charisma and force of his personality over rode all that. I had seen him several times on television and found him brilliant and original. He had a wonderful way of making me feel like I was not only the most interesting, but the only person in the world. He looked into my eyes and must have detected my unhappiness and vulnerability. The whole time, there in front of everyone, he was making love to me with his eyes, his words, and his intellect. I was smitten. He started to visit us at home and came to my showroom to take me out to lunch. Michael never bothered about it. He was never jealous. Why be jealous of someone you no longer love?

Dani, my eldest, was struggling with Dyslexia. It was not yet well-known and I turned to Brian for advice. Before becoming a full-time politician, he had been president of the Oxford Union and became a university lecturer. He met my son and told me that in a few months he could assure me the boy would be academically brilliant. *"How can you tell?"* I asked. He told me, *"When Michelangelo was asked how he could carve such wonderful images from a piece of marble, he replied, 'All I do is see the angel in the marble.'"*

He really did appeal to my most sensitive mother instinct. I would do anything to help my child. Brian made a bargain with me while having a drink at a pub near my showroom. We would go to Paris for a weekend and upon our return he would tutor Dani full-time. He professed to be in love with me, saying he would rather sleep with me than become prime minister." If you really love me put it in writing!" I said. He wrote the following on a page from a magazine. I often wondered why I kept it.

Note written by Brian Walden

We booked our flights for the following weekend and I went home, fully intending to go to Paris with him. That night I sat and watched "Casablanca" on television. I cried through the film and later called Brian to tell him I couldn't do it to my husband. I never heard from him again. He is still alive, but very old now. My angel in the marble has since become a very talented writer.

Gordon Preston

I met Gordon—my third and I hope final husband—at a labor party political activist's home. Hampstead was a wealthy, intellectual, liberal enclave in North London. It was a typical rich champagne cocktail party. There were lots of artist, actors, and professors. Zvia, sculptor friend from Israel, came with a silent blond man dressed in black who sat observing, not saying very much at all. I always think the silent types are very intelligent or very stupid, incapable of engaging in public. This man intrigued me, and I asked Zvia about him. She said, *"Oh, he just got back from fighting in the Israeli war, not Jewish, speaks Hebrew, but anyway he is gay."*

Afterwards some of the people from the cocktail party came over to my house. Gordon came too. Zvia assumed he was gay because he had not reacted when she and subsequently her younger sister made passes at him. He lived around the corner from my house and started popping in asking about the local library, borrowing books, and generally being there often. We were attracted to each other, and during dinner parties we made love with our eyes. Feeling mischievous, I once asked him in front of everyone, "Gordon, do you take off your glasses when you make love?" He did not miss a beat. "It depends," he answered.

Gordon has just returned from living in and fighting for Israel. He was somewhat shell-shocked and suspicious of me. In my car one night, we were parked and listening to an adagio by Albinoni. He asked

At country house

me, *"What do you want from me? Who are you working for?"* He thought I was possibly spying for someone. He was so involved in the work he was doing for Israel. How could I tell him I wanted to hold him, to be loved by him, to feel wanted again, to feel alive again. I was thirty-seven, a dangerous time in a woman's life, when youth seems to be finite and there is a great surge of passion, before it is too late.

In a last ditch attempt to try and rekindle my now dying marriage I told Michael that I was very attracted to Gordon. I naively thought that Michael would talk to him and somehow try to put an end to him being around. Instead he said, *"Why don't you go away with him for a weekend and get him out of your system?"* I was both terribly hurt by the fact that he cared so little for me. At the same time, I was elated to be given permission to love Gordon in the full sense of the word. I believe in being truthful in a marriage. Here I was given permission to do what I so fervently desired.

We went to Bath, a beautiful old city with great architecture, Roman baths, and Georgian crescents. The

Country house

whole place is magical. Yes, I did go away for a weekend and came back passionately in love. Michael didn't want to give me a divorce but acquiesced to let me spend Tuesday nights with Gordon. I lived for Tuesdays. The rest of the time I was eaten up with jealousy thinking that Gordon would tire of seeing me once a week and end up with someone who was free to be with him. At this point, Michael and I moved to a country house in Hertfordshire, an hour's commute from London. I thought the boarding school that Dani was at would provide a better education for the younger boys too.

They all became day students at *"St. Christopher,"* a progressive private school.

I loved the house. The business was booming. The boys were happy at their school. I bought a horse and new cars. I had everything, but I was very unhappy. Michael did not love me and I wanted to be with Gordon.

I asked Yoram, in whom I had been confiding, to meet Gordon for lunch. I was curious about his opinion. He called me and said, "He is a very good man, a bit young perhaps, but with you my dear he will age rapidly." I introduced Gordon to the boys and watched them interact. Everyone liked him.

The culmination of my power as a woman was manifested during a Passover dinner at my house. Yoram, my ex husband, Michael, my current husband, and Gordon, my future husband, were at the table with my boys. It was a raucous, tipsy dinner. Gordon, the only non-Jew, was conducting the ceremony solemnly in Hebrew. Eventually, he too got tipsy and everyone seems to have had a good time. I have never felt more loved and wanted. I selfishly basked in my triumph.

There was a revolution in Portugal and I was afraid they would confiscate our holiday villa, empty and owned by foreigners. So I asked Yoram to go and stay there for a few months. He was delighted. He loved the sun and he needed

Home in Portugal

to work on his new novel. The house was beautiful. He could work there without distractions, and I even hired a maid to come in once a week. Money was not an issue. I was rich and could afford to support him. I never saw him alive again.

A few weeks after he arrived I got a phone call from the maid. Yoram was found dead. Apparently he made a great dinner and entertained the Israeli consul. After he left, Yoram decided to have a bath. Days later he was found on the bathroom floor, dead, the water still running. It filled up the house, the sunken living room, and started flowing out onto the street behind the house.

The police came and broke down the door. After transporting him to the hospital they sealed him into a black wooden coffin with a big cross on the top. When we arrived, the hospital said that he died of either a heart attack or a brain hemorrhage. They said the results were inconclusive because the body was lying in the water in the hot summer for several days before he was found. To this day I don't believe them. At that time there were several suspicious deaths in Portugal due to faulty unventilated water heating units. I think it was a cover up to avoid damaging tourism. Yoram was fifty years old. I was next of kin, much to the surprise of the Portuguese authorities. An ex-wife making funeral arrangements in a country where divorce was unknown was shocking.

Michael came with me. Dani, at sixteen, was the only son old enough to attend a Jewish funeral. We found a rabbi who made the arrangements in the Jewish cemetery in a poor area of Lisbon. We needed a "Minyan" (ten adult Jewish men) for the service. The poor little rabbi managed to gather a bunch of ancient, doddering, old men. When the coffin was brought to the gravesite, I realized they had chipped off the cross but had no time to touch up the paint. As a result, the coffin had a big, light, unpainted cross on it. Dani was sobbing uncontrollably. The old men tried to lower the coffin into the grave. It slipped from their feeble hands and the coffin went in headfirst, vertically. At this point I started laughing. Yoram would have loved this! Eventually, some other helpers came. Finally the coffin was in the grave and Yoram was buried. When we returned to the holiday villa we found all the dirty dishes. Yoram never did tidy up in his life or death.

The photograph we found in Yoram's wallet

Yoram my Love,

Driving home last night I spoke to you again. I frequently do when I drive alone at night on the back roads. I feel your presence in the back seat. It comforts me to know that you are still with me. You have been dead now for thirty-five years. It seems so long ago. I can barely remember your face, but I can still feel your hand in mine. You know, both our son Miki and granddaughters Lexie and Cavanagh have your hands. When I touch their hands it is like touching you. Your hands were so soft.

Last photograph of Yoram

I still miss you and think of you almost daily. When you died I lost my best friend, my soul mate, and my intellectual guide. I often wonder if it is because we both came from towns so close to one other and our childhoods were so similar. Had the war not happened would we have found each other? I often wonder to what extent the concentric circles of the Holocaust will go on affecting our family. I still don't really belong anywhere. Our sons don't either. I want someone to say "Kadish" for me when I die. Perhaps if I had stayed in Israel our boys would not float about like corks in the sea—uprooted and unanchored like me.

When I left Israel and you, seven months pregnant, I didn't intend to end our marriage. I mourned all I had lost, and felt alone without you. I was resentful that you let me go with my big belly, our son Dani, and a small suitcase. Why didn't you fight for me? Why didn't you leave me with your parents and go work in the mines in Timna? We needed the money. But you said you're a writer and not a miner.

I felt devastated when I gave birth to Miki without you. I was sad that you were not there to see your new son. I wanted to take care of you, and make good all the tragedies and neglect of your childhood. You needed my compassion as much as I needed your intellect and friendship. When you finally came to visit me in Italy, the boys were in the mountains staying with a friend. We were going to see them the next day. You didn't seem to care. I was upset when you said, "It's all right, we'll see the boys tomorrow or the day after, whenever." You really came to see me and not them. Yet children adored you. You told wonderful stories to our friends' children. You paid attention to those children. Yet you never could bond with your own boys in the same way.

I am not angry with you. I understand that you were not able to rise to your parental responsibility. Perhaps because of your fractured childhood you were never exposed to how a father should behave. Even after I left, I felt protective towards you. I almost felt responsible for you. People still don't understand why I never speak about you with anger. You understood that love can transcend normal human behavior and make its own rules and concepts. I loved you until you died and beyond. It is just that we could not live within the accepted normal sense of a marriage.

After my suicide attempt you came to London to look after me. I was overjoyed and hoped that I could let the nanny go and that you would look after the boys. But you were reluctant and sat watching television all day. I became upset and when I found you taking a driving lesson outside the apartment blew up. I asked you to leave. You went to stay first with some friends and then to Hampstead in a small apartment where you stayed until you went to Portugal. Forgive me for this. I should have been more patient. You must have been ill. Eight years later you died. I wish I had taken better care of you.

One Christmas you had absolutely no money and could not buy presents to put under the tree for the boys. I still don't understand why I refused to "lend" you any money to buy presents. Perhaps it was to teach you a belated lesson? Forgive me, my love. I am still ashamed of this and will go to my grave regretting my actions.

When I married Michael, you charmed his family too. You charmed everybody. You were invited to cook fabulous dinners where you entertained all and sundry with your great skill as a raconteur. In the pubs young girls hung on your every word. You published your book, but there was not much money coming from it. I didn't mind helping you. At this time I was rich, and I could afford it. I used to come and see you to complain about my marriage. I'd ask you, "Is this what the rest of my life will be like?" You told me that things will get better and I always came away happy from these meetings. Then I fell in love with Gordon and arranged for you to have lunch with him. You called me and said : "He is a bit young, but with you my love, he will grow old rapidly."

You told Gordon that life with me will not be easy but he will never be bored.

I still feel very guilty for sending you to Portugal—guilty for your lonely and untimely death. I had a stone put on your grave in Hebrew. All it says is "Yoram Matmor, Israeli Writer." All I have left of you—your pipe, glasses, and bow tie—are in a little box in my closet. But I have our sons. Your legacy and marvelous intellect lives in them. They write like you, have your zany sense of humor, your looks, and your gestures. Both your grand-daughters have inherited not just your amazing intellect, but also your hands. When I hold their hands it feels like holding your hand, and the love overwhelms me. In them you live. I will always love you and miss you.

Yoram died in Portugal in 1976.

After we came back from Portugal, Gordon followed me out to Hertfordshire and bought a little house in the next village. I drove over to see him whenever I could. My life with Michael was unraveling. Working together was more and more difficult. Gordon took me to Scotland to his cousin's wedding. We went in great style, put my Morgan car on the train and took a sleeper for the trip. In Scotland we stayed at the famous Glen Eagles Hotel. We went to a very posh wedding where the guests were announced as they entered. Gordon's father asked me how I wanted to be announced. *"Mrs. Phillips,"* as that was my name. He then asked me why I wasn't divorced yet. *"My husband refuses to give me a divorce for the time being,"* I answered. He replied, *"That's it then!"* I was devastated. Gordon had the biggest row he and his father ever had. He told him he was going to spend the rest of his life with me, married or not, and if that meant a breach in their relationship so be it.

A few weeks later, Dad, as I ended up calling him, arrived at my showroom unannounced. He came to apologize to me. For the proud man that he was it must have been very hard. We went out and sat in a park enjoying the unusually nice weather. He told me that, as in all families, there was a skeleton in their closet too. His father, Gordon's grandfather, had a child at age seventy with a young maid. I started laughing and seeing Dad's shocked reaction I told him. "What a great recommendation for the family's virility!" At this he started to laugh with me and we became very close spending time together whenever time allowed. He was a wonderful stubborn but loving, intelligent man. I miss him still.

VISIT TO THE OLD LADY

I decided to visit Israel with Dani who was very depressed after his father's death. Gordon came with us. I was apprehensive not knowing how my old friends would receive me. How and where would I fit in after more than a decade?

We flew El-Al and, as the plane started its descent, the passengers all broke into song *"Heveynu Shalom Alechem"* (we brought you peace). My emotions got the better of me and I couldn't stop the tears. Everything came flooding back, my youth, my loves, my triumphs, my sorrows—but above all, I was coming home.

Despite my fears, everyone received me with

Visit of the
"Young Lady"

open arms. All my old friends made me feel like time had stopped and nothing changed between us. The three of us were at Tomi and Shula's home. I met their daughter Michal again. The baby I knew had grown into a lovely young woman. It was so good to see them all again. One of my old journalist friends wrote an article in her paper about my trip, calling it "The visit of the young lady." This was a play on the title of Durematt's *The Visit of the Old Lady.*

I was overwhelmed by my old friends' warmth and acceptance. I reconnected with my dear sister-in-law and her whole wonderful family. Gerti has always stood by me unconditionally—never judging, always accepting—through my divorce from her brother, my subsequent two marriages, and the birth of my two youngest boys. She visited me in every country I lived in, and kept in loving touch until her death of cancer. She was the sister I always longed for.

We travelled in the desert, climbed Masada, and again marveled at the variety of experiences the tiny country could offer. We stayed at Gordon's kibbutz and I finally met Anina, his adopted Israeli mother. I connected with her on a level I have only been able to do with Jewish women of my own background and generation.

Twelve years had passed since I left Israel and the country had changed beyond recognition. Although my close friends were the same, the mood, the politics, and the general atmosphere were completely different. It had become more like other countries—more mercenary, less tolerant and much more bellicose than before. It was not my Israel anymore.

Despite this, I longed to stay there. I felt it was my duty to stay in Israel and try to change things for the better. I felt guilty that I was leaving again. It was a cop out and I felt immense shame. I was letting my country down, taking the easy way out, and going back to where I was still a "foreigner." I was taking the coward's way out again—running away, going back to a less involved, less problematic, and easier existence. But alas, we had to go back to England. My whole life was there. I left with a heavy heart. On the plane going back there was no singing, just immense sadness.

LONDON AGAIN

Michael finally found a girl—much younger than him—and fell in love with her. We sold the horses and the country house and I moved with Gordon to a big house in Hampstead. The house needed major renovations but ended up beautiful. Michael bought an apartment in London too and moved in with his girlfriend. He still didn't want to give me a divorce and though we worked together it was getting very difficult.

I became pregnant but had to go with Michael to New York to buy materials for the next collection. I don't know where Michael was when I started hemorrhaging and had myself driven to a hospital. I was standing at the reception desk with blood pooling around my feet. A gum chewing, bored nurse, took down my credit card information. At last she called for a wheelchair and handed me a hospital card with a hole in one corner. *"Why the hole?"* I asked. *"Oh, that's to tag your toe in case you die."* She answered. They didn't have a room yet and left me on a gurney in the corridor for hours. Finally, Michael came to tell me he had to fly back to London. His girlfriend didn't like to be alone on the weekend. I begged him to stay a few days longer, but to no avail. He flew home the next day.

In London, I had to stay in hospital because I was in danger of miscarrying. When I was four and a half months pregnant I lost the baby. I was in a hospital ward. During visiting hours, I went into labor. It was very rapid. They drew the curtain around me and when the birth was over I insisted on seeing the baby.

I am holding the bowl in my hands, like a chalice. The tiny little boy lies dead—white, motionless, the color of fine parchment. He looks perfect. I open his little hand with a finger. The tiny cold hand with its perfect little nails seems to curl around my warm finger. I feel empty, almost detached from reality. I examine my little son's body almost in a clinical way. I am curious and detached. I hand the bowl back to the nurse. She takes it away.

Grief hits me next day. Gordon holds me and it is the first time I see him cry. I love him very much and am suddenly desperate to give him a child. I cannot seem to conceive again, maybe because I am almost forty years old.

I am finally pregnant again, but I develop gestational diabetes and start to bleed. The doctor I go to, Dr. Pinker, is the royal family's gynecologist. I am sent to him because of my age and possible complications. He is the best. He works three days a week in the state hospital and the rest of the time he is with his private patients. He decides I need to be in a hospital bed for a while. I decide against a private room and ask to go into a ward. I am not ill or in pain, and staying in bed is so boring. I'd rather be with other women. I observe Dr. Pinker with his patients. He lavishes the same dedicated care on every woman in his care, rich or poor. There is no difference.

Finally, Dr. Pinker decides to let me go home so long as I stay in bed. I move my workroom with my sample machinist and my cutter to the large basement of my house. They put a day bed down for me and I am only allowed upstairs to sleep. I am very happy to be working. It is saving my mind. I feel happy, excited, but bovine. All I concentrate on is designing beautiful garments. I am succeeding beyond my wildest dreams. I create the most beautiful dresses of my career—pastel chiffons with macramé trim, dyed to match, floating, dreamy creations. I am happy and serene and looked after by my wonderful Filipina Veronica, who can't wait for the baby, having been disappointed by the death of the previous little boy.

Michael finally consents to a divorce. Gordon rushes to make arrangements for our wedding at Hampstead Town hall.

At Hampstead Registry Office

Wedding

A friend brings me an exotic Afghan wedding dress. I am able to fit in it at seven months and the doctor allows me to get up for the occasion. In the limousine on the way to the wedding one of the boys asks me, "Are you excited?" Miki answers for me, "No, she is used to getting married." I have an enormous bouquet of roses that I hold in front of me before the ceremony. The registrar stares and asks, *"Are you the bride?"* *"Yes,"* I answer, *"I decided to make an honest man of him."* The cold official doesn't crack a smile and performs the boring ceremony. We go home to our house where Veronica and her friends prepared a beautiful spread for the guests. I am surrounded by parents, close friends, and a happy new husband—very much in love. I recline on the living room sofa like a queen and feel totally fulfilled. My three boys are all with me, all happy and approving. Work is going well. I have more money than I need. The next baby will be born into wealth and comfort. What else could I possibly want? It all seems so long ago. I look at a photograph from the wedding. Our parents are dead, and so are most of my old friends. The baby my best friend carries in the picture died soon after birth and I no longer live in my dream house.

Because I had to stay in bed, Gordon went on our honeymoon without me. He took the three boys to ski in Spain and came back a bit shell-shocked. It can't have been easy for a thirty-three-year-old bachelor, playing father to three boys aged nineteen, fifteen and eleven.

The birth took place in St. Mary's hospital, an old but spotlessly clean establishment. Because of my health problems, an expert on diabetes stood by. Gordon hated every minute of it. He sat at my head, but I was worried that he couldn't handle it. I wanted him to be there. After all, he married me with three children. He needed an accelerated introduction to fatherhood and I was hoping it would be a bonding experience. The

Me, Jonathan, my mother, and Gordon

birth was fast and uncomplicated. I was given an epidural and felt little pain. As soon as the baby was delivered, Dr. Pinker took it to the window and after long and careful examination turned around smiling, "Congratulations, you have a healthy baby boy," he said.

My hospital room was so full of flowers that I started sending some to the other wards. I was feted, appreciated, and loved. The collection I designed while pregnant sold more than ever in forward orders. What could possibly go wrong?

There is a rare magic moment in life, when all the gods of creation come together in perfect harmony. The stars and the universe line up. It is a moment of cosmic perfection. That was my moment.

I was still young, beautiful, loved—no, not loved, adored. Gordon was my great new love. There was a beautiful new baby, the fruit of our love and passion. My boys were still at home, still mine, still biddable, in a beautiful house surrounded by success and financial security. I was in full flight with the most amazingly well received collection, which sold a million pounds—in full possession of my power as a woman, fertile, invincible. That was my life in Thurlow Road.

My house on Thurlow Road

But things did go wrong. The situation at work became very difficult. Michael married his girlfriend. She became very jealous of the friendly relationship I had with Michael and his family. She was obsessively critical of everything I did. She would ask Michael to show her my work in the evenings and criticize my designs. Michael viewed her as an expert on fashion and started to give me a hard time. Everything I did was ridiculed and belittled and the hostility was palpable. She was buying expensive French clothes and Michael would bring them in to show me how I should design. Designing is a very insecure occupation at the best of times and I was getting very frustrated. I complained to my ex-mother in law, Laura, about the harrasment I was subjected to. She said, "Michael is the boss and she is the boss's wife. You just have to put up with it!" I felt it was totally unfair. I had worked so hard to turn this company into the little gold mine it had become. I put in six, sometimes seven days a week while the family went on vacations. My life was the business, and now the "boss's wife" will judge everything I do. No, I had to save my pride, and my soul, my integrity.

The final straw came when I found a photo of my new baby, above my desk, slashed with a pen. This was sick, and I wanted no part of it. The situation was becoming untenable.

I need a good lawyer. I call my friend Bernard. When I get him on the phone, he says, "I knew you'd call sooner or later." Although I was the goose that laid the golden eggs, I was a minority shareholder in the company with only eleven percent, which gave me no power. I went to consult my wise old boss, Mishi. "Offer to buy the company for eight hundred thousand pounds" (about a million and a half dollars), he advised. "But Mishi," I said, "I have no such money. How can I offer it?" He said, "Just do as I say, make the offer and see what happens!" The next morning we met at the company lawyer's posh office. After prolonged wrangling, I slammed my briefcase onto the table and said, "I am willing to buy you out for eight hundred thousand pounds cash here and now! Take it or leave it!"

They huddled in a corner for a few minutes, came back, and offered to buy me out for a hundred thousand pounds, which was not only fair, but a lot of money. The details were to be worked out later. So this was how poker was played, a game I never played, but I won.

In the cab Bernard asked me where I got the money. *"What money?"* I asked. I opened the briefcase, which contained some books to give it weight. Bernard went pale. *"What if they agreed to take the money and asked you to open the case?"* I answered, *"But they didn't, did they? It merely established the worth of my holdings as wise old Mishi figured it would.*" They obviously thought Mishi and Frici gave me the money to buy the company, and to this day this is the first time I tell the story.

I was banned from setting foot in the company that I gave my life to for so many years. It was painful. After staying home for a while I went to work for one of our competitors. Jean Allen was a long established very elegant firm, run by Mr. and Mrs. Parry-Billings, a late middle-aged very snobby couple. He sat in his office, waited on hand and foot, while his wife toiled in her cold basement design room. It was a strange relationship. They had been making clothes for royals in the past, and there were photos of them hobnobbing on their yacht with the Duke and Duchess of Windsor. The whole place had yellowing pictures of past glories, long dead celebrities, and a long dead racehorse they had owned. The whole place had seeds of old elegance that was somewhat shabby in the corners. The fashion shows for the buyers were run to music with Parry Billings doing the commentary. My dresses were selling very well. I was excited in a back room adding up an order when Jean admonished me, "Miss Kati, you do not have the right to add up orders, you are merely a designer here, and a junior one at that. This is not your company!" It felt like a slap in the face. I was mortified and sat crying when the owner of a factory who had worked for me in the past happened to walk in. He embraced me and I knew he felt very sorry for me. I felt utterly humiliated. I decided I could not work for someone else again, not after having been my own boss for so long.

I decided to stay home and raise my new baby. I was getting payments from my old company in partial installments. Of course, I ended up not getting all of it. The gold mine I left quickly became the victim of bad management. Michael's new young wife, having married a rich man started living a very excessive lifestyle— holidays in expensive trendy places, expensive clothes, and the bad advice on what the designs should look like. Anything that wasn't French, or at least very expensive, was deemed to be of inferior design. They hired a very sweet competent designer who produced very serviceable garments, but somehow the soul of the company was missing. The staff from my old firm kept visiting me, complaining about the new regime. I was not able to do anything about it. They probably felt I had abandoned them after all the good years we worked so hard together. Gone were the good old days where I had the power to really help them.

When the company was doing so well, I was able to actually assist people financially. I gave regular raises, paid for abortions, paid for the private education for one of the children, bought an oboe for a very talented child, paid for a divorce lawyer, and started the beginnings of a profit sharing system. I felt responsible for all these people. When I was made to leave the company I felt tremendous guilt. Maybe it seemed to them that it all happened because I fell in love and wanted to leave Michael for another man. I couldn't explain to them what went on for so long. To an extent, yes, I put my life first. I could have given up Gordon, stayed with Michael, "made do" like so many generations of women before me, but I still believe that we have one life, and it is up to us to change it. I feel guilty about my son Jonathan who was the real victim here. But would it have been better for him to grow up with an utterly miserable mother and a kind but distant father?

My children were very happy with Gordon who paid a lot of attention to them. He played with Jonathan and took him for rides on his "Triumph" motorcycle, which of course the boy loved and I hated.

Miki was often sick, and one day he was upstairs in his room with a fever when all hell broke loose. Gordon's father was visiting and I was getting ready to go to the Opera with a little girl, an exchange student from Germany. I also had to help Dani pack because he was going to Israel the next day. The phone rang, an Israeli girl we knew called Effie was on the line. *"I have to come over to talk to you urgently"* she said. I explained I was on my way out, and asked her to tell me what she wanted on the phone. *"Dani and I got married yesterday,"* she said. I told her to come over at once. Effie was a very attractive thirty-three year old woman. She needed a British passport and just married my nineteen-year-old son! I was in a total state of shock when the doorbell rang, and there she stood. I yelled up the stairs, *"Dani, your wife is here."* When Miki heard this he staggered down from bed saying, *"Please call the doctor. I am hallucinating. I just heard something about Dani's wife."* At this point I went into the living room and announced Effie's news to Gordon and his father. As an Englishman reacts in a crisis, Dad announced he is going to *"make a cup of tea."* I went to the Opera in a complete daze. To this day I have no memory of what we saw. I was in a total state of shock. Dani left for Israel the next morning and I pondered what could be done.

I was totally lost without work. I had never got up in the morning not having a definite job to do and felt completely empty. Gordon was working for a company owned by a charming group of bright young Lebanese men. They supplied electromechanical and building materials to the booming middle-eastern countries, mainly in the Gulf states. Gordon travelled a lot for the company and I worried about him somehow divulging his past in Israel. He still had nightmares about the war and cried out in his sleep in Hebrew. What if someone overheard him? He could lose his life.

The company he worked for decided to relocate to the United States and made Gordon an offer he couldn't refuse. I sat down with the boys, including Dani, and discussed moving to America. Effie wanted nothing to do with her new "husband" and Dani seemed devastated. Jonathan was having difficulties making friends. Miki was out with friends all the time. The move was deemed to be a good idea by all.

I had for many years, a sort of love hate relationship with Europe. I longed for the all enveloping order and security I imagined it being the place of my childhood. Solid substantial brick buildings, ordered, quiet, clean, tree lined streets, cobblestones worn smooth by generations who walked on them before me, the feeling of permanence and safety. Of course this was a reality I remembered and longed for, possibly only imagined as all of it blew apart so suddenly. The houses fell, the trees were uprooted, the order and security turned to murder and terror. My Daddy was ripped from me, the family, the house, the friends, the feeling of safety and permanence were gone, there was only my mother left of my former life…

Anti Semitism was on the rise again, this time it had a new name: *"Anti Zionism"*. Yes, there are a lot of things wrong in Israel, when the dream of utopia became a reality like other countries, the problems became those of ordinary countries, but of course Jews were always held to higher standards. So it is easy to say: *"I am not anti-semitic, but I hate the Zionists"*. So it is all right to hate every Jew who lives in Israel, after all, it is not considered racism or prejudice, let us hate those Jews freely again.

While writing this, there are resurgent neo-Nazis all over Europe, and it is crowded enough to bump into it frequently.

I wanted my sons to live in a cleaner world, large enough to find their place devoid of hatred and danger. I wanted them to live in a country where everyone has different ancestors, different religions and a political system where a murderous dictator would not be able to annihilate millions. It is by no means a perfect country, but the diversity is such that one is able to find a niche.

So sadly as many before us, we left the old world and came to America.

IX.
AMERICA

We had two households to pack up, two pianos, furniture, four children, two old parents, a cat and a dog. We were so busy getting everything into a forty-foot container that I barely had time to say goodbye to everyone I loved in England.

I had legal battles with Michael to allow Jonathan to come with us. I had to pay quite a lot of money and sign papers promising to send him to England to visit and keep him in private schools.

We finally left by plane and arrived in New York. It was like a traveling circus. When the cat and the dog saw us they were overjoyed. We bought a pretty house in New Jersey, around the corner from Gordon's boss, who by now made him a junior partner and we started to settle in. I have always longed for a man to keep me, and here I was, living the American dream in affluent Upper Saddle River. Yet this was the most unhappy period in my life. I hated every minute of it.

All my life I felt in control. I was the one who pushed the button that started the machine humming every day, and now there was no button and no machine. I lived in a place where people cared more about the appearance of their lawns than the state of their family, where you couldn't hang out washing or park a third car if you only had a two car garage. I was invited into homes by well-groomed women whose main worry was to make sure their drapes matched their upholstery, and where appearances meant everything. These pampered women reminded me so much of *The Stepford Wives* that I felt I was in an unreal, imaginary world. I lived for the school buses that brought the boys home and the postman who brought me letters from London. I was very homesick and started every day with a stiff drink.

I found a lump in my breast and flew back to London to see my doctor. We had been in America such a short time that I felt more comfortable there. I left the children with Gordon and a nanny and went to stay with a friend. At the cancer hospital they gave me my X-rays and told me to take them to the surgeon without opening the envelope. Of course, in the cab I had a look and saw the lump they called "suspicious."

I was in my private hospital room waiting for my surgeon the night before my operation when Dani, who was visiting London, came with a friend to have a shower in my bathroom. They brought me a tiny bottle of champagne and after their showers sat on my bed in their underwear and towels. When the surgeon came he looked a bit shocked. I told him with bottle in hand, "I decided to celebrate with these nice young men, after all who knows what the future will bring?" I also told him that if the lump was malignant, not to take off my breast until I was awake to make the final decision.

When I awoke from the operation I immediately felt for my breast, which was where it was before. The lump turned out to be benign. This was my first brush with cancer. I flew back to America accompanied by Dani.

My son Jonathan decided that he was unhappy in America and begged to go back to live with his father. It broke my heart to see him go through to the waiting room at the airport. Every time the school bus drove by in the afternoon, I sat and cried for the son I missed so much. I was worried about this child who was so affectionate and needed so much love. Would he get it with Michael and his cold English wife? He was only twelve and still very needy.

Miki graduated high school a year early and decided to do nothing at all. I insisted he get a job or go to college. As a result, he disappeared into the lower East side of Manhattan. After a lot of trials and tribulations he notified us that he joined the U.S. navy. We flew to Chicago for his ceremony for graduating from boot camp. It was a surreal experience, very unfamiliar, very American.

Dani, after a divorce from Effie, decided to go to college in New Jersey. He also had a job as night security guard at Minolta's headquarters. This ended when someone stole the hotline telephone off his desk while he was doing the nightly rounds in the deserted, dark building. He then decided to become an actor and got hired by a children's touring theatre company called the "Robin Hood Players" based in Arizona.

The business in London went bankrupt. I flew back and bought it from the receivers and made the mistake of putting two of my old employees in charge. One was a very good salesman and the other ran the office and finances for a number of years before the debacle. I made the mistake of thinking good employees would make good leaders and bosses. Unfortunately leadership is a trait you cannot learn. Neither of them had it. Furthermore, they had no people skills and became rather too bossy. I also bought Jean Allen's business, which folded around the same time. I flew over twice a year to put together a collection and it broke my heart to see poor lady-like Jean Allen suffering under my partners. By this time P.B., her husband, was too ill to work and could not be left at home alone either. So she sat him in a corner in the workroom where she could watch him. Eventually, a rich aunt of Jean's died and left her a house and money in one of the Channel Islands. They retired there.

The business in London was not doing well. I was trying to run it as an absentee landlord. My partners had no idea how to manage and eventually we closed it with a huge loss of my funds.

I was stuck at home with a very lively toddler who was systematically demolishing the house while I sat and cried. I longed for some interaction with grown-ups—real people and not the "Stepford Wives" I met. I found a daycare for baby David and joined the local volunteer ambulance corp. The training was rigorous and very interesting, and the people I met there were real. They were from the families who lived there before Upper Saddle River became a posh suburb. Through my work on the ambulance I got to see the seamy underside of this fake wealthy fantasy world. Some men who lost their job would pretend to go to work every day and eventually sat in their garage and killed themselves with carbon monoxide. Wives would overdose when a husband left them for a woman younger than their daughters. Old people lived in solitude without anyone looking in to see if they were okay.

We were called by the police to a house where a poor old couple lived behind closed doors in total squalor. The wife in her eighties was lying on a bed covered by newspapers that absorbed the pus oozing from her gangrenous legs. She died two days later. This kind of thing doesn't happen in poorer areas where people live in much closer proximity and know what goes on with their neighbors. We were called to patch up victims of domestic violence, transported dead mafia types from very luxurious homes, and dealt with hysterical and drug addicted rich people. Parents would indulge their teenagers by buying them new sports cars the day they graduated high school. Every weekend there were horrendous and often fatal accidents involving young people. Speed and alcohol was the cause. The ambulance stood by during football games. This is where I learned to despise this brutal game that left so many beautiful young men injured. I also learned to hate drunks, especially after attending a young nurse who lost both legs in a head on crash. She was driving home from a night shift when a drunk drove into her car. He walked away unhurt.

When you are in a ditch upside down, covered in someone's blood, trying to keep someone alive, life takes on a different meaning. Finally, I found some people I could talk to. These were the real good Americans and found over the years. I found that there are actually many people like that.

My health was not great and I had to have a hysterectomy. By this time I had good medical contacts in the U.S. and had my surgery in New Jersey. The surgery went well, but I got an infection afterwards and had to stay in hospital for several days. I was convinced I was going to die. I called a nurse and told her I wanted to donate my body to medical research. She told me I would have to pay two hundred dollars for administrative fees. I was outraged and decided to leave notes under my hospital pillow and mattress making sure my wishes would be carried out. I never removed the notes. I wonder if some poor person's body was given away instead of mine.

During my stay at the hospital I had a strange experience. I was asleep, attached to monitors and the IV when I woke up seeing both Yoram and my dead real father at the foot of my bed. They were young, healthy, and dressed alike in beige silk turtleneck sweaters and beautiful beige cashmere jackets. I was so happy to see them so well and healthy. They smiled at me and told me to come with them. They had their arms open to receive me. I got out of bed, removed the IV and the other monitors and started to join them. But I changed my mind. I started screaming, saying I had a lot to do and couldn't leave yet. The nurses came running and I told them to tell Yoram and my father I didn't want to go. I pointed to them but the nurses saw nothing. I fell asleep.

Dani arrived and told me he wanted to start a theatrical touring company like the one he worked for. He showed me a leaflet. He had just printed leaflet describing "The Hampstead Players." "How much did you pay for this?" I asked.

"Eighty Dollars," he answered. "You just wasted eighty dollars," I told him. Boy, was I wrong! Our little theatre company has become very successful!

I didn't see enough of Gordon. He was working long hours and traveling a lot. I was depressed and still very homesick. I was also worried about his business. It seemed to be sailing too near the wind, both legally and financially. I gave Gordon an ultimatum. Either we went back to England, or we would stay in the United States, buy a farm, and retire together. At this point, we had enough money saved and interest rates were very high. I always wanted to try to live in the country and be self-sufficient.

We looked for a house with land. We wanted to be no more than two hours from an international airport, near mountains so Gordon could ski, and close to the sea because we wanted to sail. I also wanted some land around the property. After looking at New York state and Vermont we found our house in New Hampshire. It was a huge old farmhouse with a large barn, but above all , it came with fifty acres of fields and woods.

BARNSTEAD

Off again, with two huge moving vans, two cars, four children, two old parents, the cat, and the dog. When we neared our new house there were wild looking hairy bikers everywhere. I was horrified. Later, we found out it was the annual biker week, when literally thousands of bikers descend on New Hampshire.

Our new house, built in 1779, was originally a working farm with a huge red barn attached by a series of rooms. We ended up converting part of the house and barn. It is wonderful what you can do with a wooden structure. Barnstead was very small at the time, with about two thousand people. It was a real learning experience living in rural America.

We moved in, bought a heifer and a little bull, some sheep, geese, ducks, chickens, and a pig. We planted a vegetable garden and started trying to "live off the land." I never worked so hard in my life. It was never ending. Looking after a farm proved to be both backbreaking and comical. Everything that could go wrong went wrong. The animals kept escaping and we were singularly unsuccessful with our attempts at trying to breed our pig, Carol. Eventually, we bought and raised a male pig, but he turned out to be the only gay pig I ever heard of. The pigs spent months together, probably discussing fashions, but no piglets! Pigs never stop growing, and Carol was getting bigger and bigger. Eventually after she reached a thousand pounds she got too heavy and got arthritis. We had to put her down, but of course you can't eat a friend, so no pork for us.

Keeping sheep was not much better. They kept getting out, devouring flowers and vegetables, and they always gave birth on the coldest nights of the year. I sat with my ewes at night dressed in several coats and helped with the births. When the lambs came out they were freezing, so I brought them into the kitchen, dried them with a hair-dryer, put little sweaters on them, and took them back to their mothers. You have to put them on the teat and teach them to suck. After this, of course, it was very hard to eat them. The beef cattle were a problem too. They came as calves and decided I was their mother. They would come running when I called them. When they grew and were butchered, I had a hard time eating the meat. The only thing I never felt guilty about eating were chickens. They are thoroughly nasty creatures and will peck a chick to death if it is not their own. The problem with having chickens was trying to stop predators. Raccoons were able to crawl under the chicken house and remove enough floorboards to get in and kill every hen. Foxes do the same. In winter the chicken house was too cold so we had to bring the hens into the barn. They had lice and we had to disinfect the barn.

Gardening was hard too. Every season different pests ate different fruits or vegetables. We did not want to use chemicals, so we shared our produce with a wide variety of pests. We cut our own hay, which in itself is a major gamble. You need at least three very dry hot days. The first day you cut, the second day you fluff and turn over the drying hay, and the third you put it in rows, bale it and put it in the barn. It sounds simple, but the equipment breaks a lot, the baling twine breaks, and, of course, it usually starts to rain when the hay bales are still on the ground.

This is where I learned about the kindness of strangers around here. When it started to rain, several neighbors—some of whom we have never met—came from nowhere and helped us pick up the hay and get it into the barn rapidly. I do have faith in the random wonderful kindness of people. I have been blessed by so much kindness, starting with the kind woman who hid me in her barn when I was a child and saved my life.

After a while, farming, though back breaking, was not enough and we started to meet people and join in the community. I joined the local volunteer ambulance crew. You really get to know people and become close friends when you are dealing with tragedy. When you are holding a dying person or injured child there is no one closer to you than your EMT partner. You rely on each other not just for the physical help, but also for the psychological support after a terrible call where you deal with blood and death. And then, of course, there is the relief of black humor, the tool to relieve the sorrow and pity.

We were called to a house on a freezing winter evening where an old bed ridden gentleman had some sort of medical emergency and needed to be transported to the hospital. The house had a series of small rooms and narrow corridors and the man was very tall and very heavy. We strapped him onto a gurney but we couldn't get him around the corners of the narrow corridor. Someone had the idea of opening the window and handing him through to the outside. The ground floor the bedroom was on, gave onto the back of the house and the sloping land was covered in a thick layer of frozen ice. As we managed to hand the gurney through the window, the people outside accidentally let go and the gurney went downhill full speed all the way, finally ending up at the bottom where it stopped next to a stone wall. The patient survived, but our reputation was in tatters.

Another call was a bit weird when our crew chief accidentally dropped an oxygen cylinder on the floor of the emergency room. Waiting for a possible explosion people disappeared in droves, leaving the patients behind.

Gordon also took classes and became a first-aid trained ambulance member. On one of his first calls, he started to unload a gurney with a patient at the hospital when another urgent call came in for a car accident with multiple injuries. In his hurry, he forgot to unhook the nasal canula attaching the man to the ambulance's oxygen supply, and only noticed it when the poor patient's nose was pulled up to his eyebrow!

Gordon also joined the fire department and started going to fires in the area. We met wonderful real selfless people. All these services were staffed by unpaid volunteers who gave so much to others for free.

We were asked by some neighbors to attend some school board meetings and found out about our school superintendent. He was largely responsible for us quickly becoming American citizens. The school system was, and still is, the largest employer in town. The superintendent had made it his personal kingdom for sixteen years. He pretty much owned the school board by bestowing largesse on its members. One of them had all the fuel contracts for the school system, another had the bus contract, and many members of their families had nice lucrative jobs in the schools. We had and elementary school. Neighboring Pittsfield had an elementary school as well as a high school, where our town sent most of our high school students. As we did not have our own high school our students were going to whichever nearby high school had space for them. This caused great hardship to the kids who never knew which school might ultimately accept them. We found out that The superintendent's daughter operated a special education company, which performed all evaluations of students. After determining the student's "needs" the company was contracted to provide "services'" to all the schools. Whether these "services" were really needed or effective nobody knows. However the expense was horrendous.

The towns pre-paid everything to the SAU (School Administrative Unit), which would at all times have at least a few hundred thousand dollars in its bank account. Because there are no taxes in New Hampshire, the property taxpayers of these small towns fund the whole cost of education. This was at a time when interest rates were at eighteen percent. The superintendent kept these funds in current checking accounts that paid no interest whatsoever. It seemed unbelievable but then the penny dropped. This man was one way or another profiting greatly from these two poor towns!

We started attending school board meetings, which are public, but he still tried to intimidate us by having us write our names down, so I would write nonsense, such as "Nemesis" or "Your worst nightmare." Sometimes he would put one of his cronies sitting next to us so we started writing rude things in Hebrew to each other and showed our notes to his befuddled spies. It was comical. The problem was that too many people depended on his generosity and he owned them. Corruption is the same everywhere. In Barnstead it was simply cheaper to buy someone.

It all came to a head when we took a whole page ad in the little local paper posing questions. "Why is the company servicing our special education needs also in charge of determining what services are needed, who needs them, and how much it costs? Why is this a private company owned by the superintendent's daughter and how does this not pose serious conflict of interest? Why are there vast sums of money in the school system's checking accounts without getting interest, while the towns have to borrow money at 18% to pre-pay for the schools?" The newspaper owner and editor questioned whether he wanted to publish it, but there was nothing illegal or slanderous. You are allowed to question any information that is public and according to freedom of speech it was totally legal.

As soon as we got home, The superintendent was on the phone. The editor must have phoned him as soon as we left his office. He wanted Gordon to come to his office "to discuss the problem in private." Gordon told him that he would like to discuss it in the Town Hall in public.

The war was on. The superintendent tried to get the two towns to buy land and build a joint high school, which would have cemented his kingdom further, and a lot of his cronies would be profiting from it. When his contract came up for renewal he held the meeting at a fancy restaurant and invited the school board to dinner at the public's expense. This is where they all voted to renew his contract.

We had no rights as green card holders, so we decided it was time to become fully voting citizens of our new country. The hearing for our citizenship was in Boston, and we were directed to two separate offices. Gordon's hearing was conducted by a nice friendly woman. They discussed sailing and politics and she stamped his papers. I knew I was in trouble when the two girls before me came out of the examiner's office sobbing. I was called and sat down in front of a grumpy middle-aged man. He took my passport and looked it for some time, noting a name change. I explained that when I married Gordon my passport was still valid, so they added my new name.

"So you are divorced. Whose fault was it? Did you commit adultery? Though shocked, I very politely asked him why this was relevant? He changed the subject and started quizzing me about the Constitution, American history, the amendments, names of all the presidents, and some vice presidents. I had studied the book for days so I scored 90% correctly. My tormentor then told me to take some dictation to see if my English was good enough. He started, "I do not wish to become a citizen of the United States of America." I put my pen down refusing to write this. I was almost in tears and decided to walk out. As I got up, he stamped my papers and told me I had passed the test. Son of a bitch! What a nasty little man! I wonder why someone who obviously hates women and immigrants should be in such a position, able to arbitrarily ruin peoples' lives. Here we go again, the nasty little bullies, given a little power or a uniform, lording it over those without power.

We started getting more and more involved in local politics. I found it fascinating to see democracy in action. Town meetings where people actually discussed, argued, and voted was a whole new experience. Wherever I lived before I didn't even know who my representatives were, let alone be able to question any decision. Yes, this is on a small scale, and sometimes people drone on just to hear themselves talk , but ultimately anyone who cares to participate has the right to vote. I hope they never change this procedure to something remote and less personal.

I was still on the ambulance and Gordon became a school board member. When he was voted chairman, he was able to get a majority of the school board to vote against renewing the superintendent's contract. This caused a lot of resentment among his cronies and we got a lot of flack. We got anonymous phone calls telling us to go back where we came from, called us flatlanders and outlanders. Late one night, a long black limousine with tinted windows drove up to the front door and sat with the engine idling. Being a bit paranoid after all the nasty messages, Gordon went out to investigate. Not knowing what to expect he held a gun to the driver's window and asked what they wanted. The window slowly wound down, and to his horror, it was a wedding party who got lost on the back roads. No apology would suffice to assuage the shock of the poor folks in the car.

My mother and step father lived with me until they died. I built them an apartment in the house with their own kitchen and bathroom, it was fine until my stepfather got Alzheimer's disease. He went downhill rapidly, started to get violent with my mother and had to be locked in his room at night so he wouldn't start a fire or flood the house. He became incontinent. When we locked his door at night he would try to break the lock because he thought he was in a gas chamber. It is tragic to see an intelligent, educated man, who could play the piano, tell me stories as a child, teach me sentences in Latin, songs in Hungarian, not remember who he was, let alone where he was anymore. It was becoming very difficult for my mother. We had to put him in a nursing home, and while driving him there I felt terrible guilt. He died soon after, calling me by hid dead daughter's name, Dita.

GABRIELLA, MY MOTHER

My mother

My mother Gabriella was an extraordinary woman. Her ability to survive was in large part due to her immense courage. She did not break under torture. She survived war and hunger. After the Russians invaded, she was able to get enough food not just for us, but for most of the people in our apartment building.

Above all, she was full of compassion and caring. I remember the poor, shuffling, bald, emaciated holocaust survivors she brought home from the train station when we waited for my father. She took these poor people in, bathed them, fed them, cried with them, clothed them, and gave them money to travel wherever they were heading to find what was left of their former life and family.

Once she brought home a beggar on crutches. He only had one leg so she made a little wooden shelf that she attached to one of his crutches, padded it with a small pillow, covered it in red velvet, and proceeded to teach the grateful man how to sit on it, resting while standing around for hours, begging.

My mother was not an intellectual, but her cleverness, resourcefulness, and ability to read people was amazing. She made a beautiful wedding dress for a young daughter of one of her employees. The poor girl died of tuberculosis and her last wish was to be buried in a wedding dress. There were shortages of materials, but she manages to find a beautiful piece of satin and sat embroidering it with pearls.

She also made a crown and veil to go with it. It was so beautiful I wanted to die just to wear such a dress.

My mother had planned to have me work with her and continue her business when she retired. It was a great disappointment to her, when I started my own business in Tel-Aviv without her. She could not understand that like her, I was stubborn and had to be my own boss. Not being allowed to pursue my dream of going to Edinburgh I wanted to be successful on my own. I did not want any part of my parents' business, I needed to be independent

She was an incredible craftsman. My mother could look at a woman and make her a garment that fitted her perfectly, without having to measure or make a pattern. She could make the most intricate dresses without any problems; she could create the most elaborate draped garments in minutes. She never had to correct anything. Everything she did was right the first time. Her taste very flamboyant; she thought nothing of decorating a garment with flowers cut out of foam rubber or sticking bits of plastic to decorate a silk dress. During her many successful years as a dressmaker, she mainly copied Paris fashions, but her own creative ideas came full circle when she made costumes for our theatre. The worked tirelessly making costumes, so well made, they still look like new decades later. Her standards were never lowered and even the week before her coma and subsequent death, she was making patterns, making sure we could carry on without her.

As my mother got older, I noticed that she started to think more and more of the past. Her smile, which she managed to get back after the war, appeared less frequently. She startled at noises and became suspicious if someone came to the door. She would ask, "Why are they here? What do they want?" She became suspicious of strangers, only trusted immediate family, and could not watch anything sad on television. Her mind was still very clear, but the past kept bothering her more and more.

As we age, the past comes clearer and closer, perhaps this is why so many Holocaust survivors end their lives by committing suicide. People like the writer Primo Levi, and the famous child psychologist Bruno Betelheim, are just two examples. When our memories overwhelm us, perhaps death is the only solution.

Mother could still get joy seeing the grandchildren. She made them all hats with ears, that, had they been a few years older, they would have been mortified to have to wear. She made hundreds of costumes and in her spare time and she crocheted many blankets. She also worried about me not wearing a coat when I went out even for a few minutes. Her hearing went, but her work ethic never diminished. I have no memory of ever seeing her hands idle.

My mother developed minor bleeding in her intestines. They were all over, and although she had an operation to correct it, new bleeding kept occurring.

There was no diagnosis as to why this was happening .The only solution was to have blood transfusions to replenish the lost blood. At first it was every three weeks, but soon it was once a week. She was not happy at the local hospital so I drove her to Dartmouth Hitchcock Hospital in Lebanon, an hour and a half away. She would frequently have to spend the night there. This went on for what seems like years. At one point she decided she didn't want any more transfusions. I still feel guilty for not having forced her to go back to the hospital, but she told me she was so tired and she couldn't face it anymore. This was on a Monday. By Wednesday she was in a coma. The wonderful caring nurses of Hospice were here several times a day, and I was giving her morphine injections to relieve any pain she might feel.

I had a hard time equating the body lying there totally unresponsive, with the huge life force that had been my mother—my all powerful, resourceful, brave, talented, original, strong, loving mother. She saved me during the war; she survived torture, lost the love of her life, my father, lived with tragedy, and stood up to the Nazis, the Russians, and the Communists. She worked day and night to carve out a niche for us in a world that collapsed all around us.

Now she was just a husk. I felt she had left her body. Her soul was no longer there. I was completely detached, almost on autopilot administering the morphine, checking her intravenous port, changing her, almost in a daze. I felt nothing. I couldn't talk to her or hold her hand. This body was not my mother. My mother was not here.

She died on Saturday when I was downstairs eating lunch.

In the afternoon, when the undertakers came to get her, my son Jonathan was with me. He told me that when they put her body on the gurney I let out a loud inhuman howl. I have no memory of it at all. I remember a feeling of almost relief. We all went out to a restaurant and had a good time. I suppose this is what wakes are supposed to be like.

The pain, the feeling of loss, the despair, hit me later. I mourned my mother, I mourned my childhood, I mourned the loss of her love, and the loss of my final connection to that whole world which no longer exists. I lost my anchor. I will forever feel terrible guilt for every harsh or insensitive word I said to her, guilt for being impatient, not wanting to take her shopping all the time, yelling at her for not using her hearing aid, being annoyed for having no freedom from the permanent responsibility of caring for her. I would like to get down on my knees in front of her and beg her to forgive me. Forgive me for not touching her, not kissing her, for not holding her hand as she lay dying.

Gordon started traveling to Russia, buying old computers and shipping them to Wales where a factory dismantled the machines and extracted the gold, which, after taking a fee, they remitted back to the Russians.

During this period the theater company continued touring, and slowly it started to grow. The original teams, which were composed of two men, were replaced by teams made of a boy and girl, which enabled us to provide greater variety. Dani, and later Miki, my two brilliantly talented writers, adapted classics and original versions of stories to suit the limits of time, travel, and ages of the students. There was not much competition and we grew and grew, until we reached over two thousand shows a year. We had ten tours from the east coast and eight tours from our west coast operation. We housed the east coast actors at the farm for three weeks of rehearsals, which were held at different local halls. Between the two venues we covered all 48 contiguous states. It was an exciting time but it needed a lot of heavy work.

We established a California office for the *"Hampstead Players"* and I went there to organize the setting up of the rooms to house the props and costumes in a space Dani was renting in Korea Town. It was a great space, but for the roaches, the size of foot stools! When I needed someone to paint the walls I drove to Home Depot where there was a large group of Mexican men, all clamoring for work. I felt really bad, but decided to hire the oldest, frailest, little man. His name was Hector who turned out to be a great worker and a really nice man. In my combination of Italian and Portuguese I managed to converse with him. I did understand everything he said. After I thanked and paid him, he took my hand and looked into my eyes. *"I need to tell you something,"* he said. *"You are a very kind woman but unfortunately you will have a great tragedy in your life. In the end it will be all right, God will help you and fix your problem."* I would soon remember his prediction.

CANCER

During my trip to California, I went to San Francisco to visit my dear friend Nigel, with whom we had wonderful times together as neighbors in London and sailing in the Mediterranean. I was sitting in his garden reading a book, when I detected a growth under my chin. As soon as I got home I immediately saw a doctor and had the tumor removed for a biopsy.

During the surgery, I heard the doctor say: *"What a pity. It has its own blood supply."* I knew then that the news was not good. In the recovery room I told the doctor what I heard. He said it was impossible, I had been unconscious. But I did hear, and after the lump was sent to the lab, he called me to his office and broke the news. *"You have metastatic neuro-endocrine cancer."* I was stunned. I had no idea what it meant exactly, except that it had already spread and no one could predict the future. How long have I got?

How would this ship, called family, navigate without me? I called Gordon, told him what I found out, and got into my car to drive home. As the diagnosis started to sink in, the sadness suddenly overwhelmed me. I could hardly see the road through my tears and had to stop the car several times. When you hear the words, *"You have Cancer,"* it is like a punch in the stomach. Time stops, everything stops. You stop thinking. You feel paralyzed and cannot breathe.

Cancer diagnosis follows the same psychological patterns as mourning. First comes the shock and disbelief. They must be wrong, other people get cancer, and it must be a mistake. My disbelief was so strong that we sent part of the lump from the operation to a lab. We wanted to make sure it was mine and not someone else's and that the original lab did not make a mistake. Unfortunately it was mine. I did have cancer.

The doctor sent me to an oncologist who was rather brusque and matter of fact. He told me he would start chemotherapy almost immediately, followed by surgery and possibly radiation. He could give me no prediction as to what might happen. He delivered what to me was a possible death sentence, in a factual, rather off hand manner. After I got home I had a few questions and called him. He wouldn't come to the phone. He was busy and didn't return my call even the next day. His whole establishment was run like an assembly line, patients in easy chairs all connected to intravenous devices.

I was uneasy and wanted a second opinion. I was sent to Massachusetts General Hospital to their endocrine cancer specialist, an old Chinese gentleman. As I walked into the treatment room, a large, very healthy cockroach followed me in. The doctor sat me down and without explanation or warning, stuck a tube through my nose into my throat. The surprise and pain shocked me to tears, whereupon he said, "No pain, no gain!" and calmly stuck another tube down my second nostril.

He then explained that he believed in surgery as his preferred treatment, so he would cut away everything under my chin, and around my throat. This would most likely result in my losing my salivary glands, hence my teeth will fall out, and I will possibly have difficulty tasting food. After all: *"No pain, no gain."* I asked what could happen if the surgery didn't get all the cancer? He told me it would probably spread to my brain, but that too could be operated on.

My confusion and despair was overwhelming. Here I was with a death sentence hanging over my head, having to choose between two very different treatments.

I finally went to Dartmouth Hitchcock Hospital in Lebanon, New Hampshire, and my life changed. The whole atmosphere of this hospital is completely different. They treat you with respect and affection, discuss all the alternatives and help you make your own decisions. Your healthcare becomes a collaborative well-informed decision and the doctor spends a long time talking about the treatment and the effect it has on the patient's mental and emotional state. My tall lovely doctor had a spectacular handlebar moustache and a charismatic kind personality. He hugged me and told me, "We will throw everything at this cancer, as long as it doesn't kill you. It should kill the cancer. It won't be easy, but it should do the trick."

I asked him what stage my cancer was. *"Fourth stage,"* he said. *"What comes after fourth stage?"* I asked. *"There are no more stages,"* he said, but told me not to worry. It will be all right, and he gave me a big hug. I felt he really cared and I trusted him. This man was a competent, caring, dedicated human being with courage to go the extra mile and try to save a life.

The doctor who saw me started out as a zoologist and went into oncology later. One time I asked if I should try to take shark fin supplements. *"Think of the poor shark,"* he said. *"Doctor,"* I said, *"If it is a choice between me and the shark, the shark dies."*

The treatment rooms were totally different from my prior experience. Each patient had a curtained area with a bed and constant attention from kind, dedicated nurses. At first they gave me the chemotherapy intravenously but soon my veins blew out and they decided to put in a "Port" on my chest with easy access to a vein without too much trouble. The first couple of treatments were not too bad, but the poison they use is cumulative, and it starts to hit you. At first your hair starts to fall out, your skin becomes dry, brittle, tears easily, and food tastes strange. Sleep becomes difficult and your mind starts to get confused.

This is the stage when sadness and fear of death hits you. You mourn for everything you will never experience in the future. Your children will not have a mother, a grandmother. Your husband will lose his wife, and there is so much to lose. You howl uncontrollably, grasp at any straws of hope, you start reading the obituary pages to see how many people die at your age or younger. You go from terror to sadness, to feeling helpless, to the need to be touched. When you have cancer people tend not to touch you. It is almost a subconscious atavistic fear of contagion, but it is a real problem. I noticed that at the hospital, the oncologists didn't wear gloves, they touched a lot and hugs were constant. It made a huge difference. My sons instinctively knew I needed affection and made it a point to cuddle and kiss me.

When I was diagnosed, because of the statistics of the disease, I was given about six months to live. My youngest son David, left college in Colorado and came home to be near me. He took me to most of my chemo treatments. Although he hates hospitals, he sat by my side patiently, for hours and hours. He drove me in his Jeep which had a hard suspension; your bottom could tell when you drove over a coin if it was heads or tails. David so proudly drove me in his beloved jeep that I didn't have the heart to tell him, how excruciating it was to be driven in it for an hour, after a five hour chemo treatment.

It is amazing that in this modern world of ours, cancer still defeats the medical profession. All they can do is slash, burn, or poison.

The first Christmas after my diagnosis all my sons and grandchildren came home. That is when my hair started falling out in clumps. Not to scare my granddaughters, I made fun of it. I pulled out a clump of hair and chased them around with it. They thought it was fun, but later I would go to my room and have a secret cry.

My son Dani brought home his lovely girlfriend to meet me. She made such a wonderful impression on me that I asked her to marry my son. I knew he would be loved and cared for after my death. At first Heidi seemed apprehensive, knowing our family history. She was concerned that her German father, who had been a soldier in the Wermacht, would become a problem for me. I put her mind at ease. At the time her father was only a teenager, and anyway I don't believe in visiting the sins of the fathers on the children.

I was getting very weak and tired from the chemo and had to lie down frequently. During lunchtime, the whole family was downstairs having fun. The laughter reverberated through the house. I was overcome by a terrible sadness, life is going on downstairs without me, and soon I will not even hear them anymore. I will be gone forever. I will not see my grandchildren grow up, two of my sons will be orphans and somehow when our mothers die, we all become orphans even if we have a father. It is true that nobody ever loves your children as unconditionally as you, except your mother. Who will give them all, the love they need, the love I have so much of in my heart, the love that soon will die with me?

I began having a recurring dream. It is night on a beach. There is a bonfire with my family having loud fun around it. I am on a raft being pulled out into the black sea by the tide. I stand up screaming for help, but nobody can hear me and I am pulled further and further into the dark sea, further from my family on the beach. I always woke up terrified, sobbing uncontrollably.

I had plans that during the times I could not get out of bed I would to read all the books I never had time to read before. Unfortunately, my brain was not working right. Nothing could hold my attention for any length of time. I could only concentrate on books about serial killers. I am not a violent person, I have no idea why these horrors kept my attention, but they did. Maybe when you are in mortal danger you need to think of someone who is a worse situation? A friend who worked in publishing sent me a box of these books that I read cover to cover. Thankfully, I do not remember any of it.

When I could get out of bed I worked regularly, thinking it was useful, not realizing I made a mess of things. Everyone around me quietly rectified the mistakes I made and didn't tell me to give it up. I was convinced I was essential to the company.

I do believe in the power of good and evil. I believe both can affect things. Evil seems to be the stronger, but the power of love is not to be discounted. I was diagnosed with cancer just before everybody was on Facebook, so people reached out to me by writing and sending cards. I got good wishes from people all over the world, especially from young actors who spent time with our company here at my home. Some people prayed for me in different places—in churches and synagogues. Some even prayed to Allah. I had a wall that was completely covered with cards and letters. I called it my wall of love. When feeling especially low, which was often, I would stand in front of my wall of love touching it, feeling all the wonderful healing energy.

After several weeks of misery and treatment I woke up one morning feeling furious. Hell no! I am not going to die! Hitler didn't get me! Cancer is not going to either! I am going to fight this disease, stop feeling sorry for myself, and stop being a cancer patient! I decided to be my old self who just happens to have cancer at the moment. I simply didn't have time to die.

I put myself on a diet, no meat, lots of tofu, red and green peppers, kale, garlic, spinach, broccoli and brown rice. I ate all kinds of mushrooms and started taking maitake mushroom pills daily. I drank gallons of unsweetened green tea, (they told me to drink a gallon of liquids a day to save my kidneys from the effect of chemo.) and more importantly, I taught myself to meditate.

It is very hard to meditate, to think of nothing. I found it was easier to concentrate on my fear of heights. Our barn has three floors with a cupola on the top which has a panoramic view all around. I closed my eyes and imagined walking through the barn, climbing up the ladder into the cupola, removing one of the surrounding windows, climbing onto the ledge and hurling myself out, my arms wide, flying. I flew around above our house and fields, over the forest, over the pond, soaring like a bird. It was a wonderful feeling of power, control, and at the same time peace, perfect peace. It got so I could do this every time I felt nausea or terror, and slowly I felt I took control of my body and my life.

The treatments were over, black fuzz grew on my head, I started feeling better, the doctors were still looking for the primary site where the cancer had originated, but slowly life returned to normal.

I have no idea what happened, but I do believe we can't even access a small fraction of our brain. Perhaps will power in this instance was simply optimism, influencing perception and it gave me peace. When at peace, the body is stronger and more able to fight. Perhaps I was lucky enough to call on things inside my body which conquered the disease. I do believe I have some powers. I can meditate my blood pressure down ten points in ten minutes. I recover fast anytime I have a cold, a cough, or an infection. When I get a cut, I heal faster than anyone I know. I have high pain tolerance and my children say I suffer from terminal optimism. Mainly, I don't think about cancer or any of the many physical problems that come with age.

The amazing thing is that surviving cancer adds incredible value to life. It is the best thing that can happen to one psychologically. The colors are brighter, the snow is whiter, every morning you wake up you rejoice, just being alive is such a high. You become more tolerant, less petty, more patient, perhaps a better person. My mantra since cancer, if anything bothers me, is: "It is not cancer." Dare I say, that in many ways, cancer is a blessing, if you survive it, of course.

I once talked to one of my boys about the fact that as I get older. I need more and more maintenance and spare parts. I am like an old car. How long does one want to invest time and money to fix an old car?: "You are not just any old car," he said, "You are a valuable vintage car."

I still go the hospital regularly. They still search for my primary cancer, and I apologize to them for screwing up their statistics.

The boring succession of age related health issues follow in quick succession, cataract surgery, blood clots, carpal tunnel surgery, erosion of cartilage in both knees, requiring shots several times a year to be able to walk. I start taking blood thinners and I can no longer eat dark green vegetables or drink my beloved green tea. Because I wake up every morning, seeing the leaves change color in the fall, pickling cucumbers in the summer, seeing my beloved grandchildren grow, I have a lot of joy in my heart. The mere fact of being alive gives me such a wonderful optimistic feeling. Every day is such a gift!

HAMPSTEAD PLAYERS

The 'Hampstead Players' stage company

I have worked full time for the *Hampstead Players* and *The Hampstead Stage Company* for thirty years. I am very proud of this, because we bring theatre and culture to children who get so little of it. It is far more meaningful than fashion. After all, enriching a child's mind it is far more important than some woman looking good wearing a dress I designed.

I am much happier doing this instead of more commercial endeavors, but of course there is not much money in theatre, and for many years we subsidized the Hampstead Players and The Hampstead Stage Company. Going from savings and no mortgage, we now have a huge mortgage on our house and no savings. Yet I have no regrets, I am much happier and more fulfilled providing enrichment to thousands of children throughout the states. In some places it is a cultural desert, children have never seen live theatre, and probably neither did their teachers. We provide real theatre, not watered down shows for younger audiences. Children are smart and discerning, and there is no need to play "down" to their level. The plays are not only well written, but intelligent, entertaining, enlightening and they carry a moral message as well. There is so much you can teach while entertaining.

One of the joys for me is the actors. We hire young professional college graduates from all over the states. These wonderful young people are talented, educated, and dedicated to their profession. In this mercenary world of ours it is so refreshing to meet young people who dedicate their lives to art and not just money. They are generally wonderful people and it is a privilege to get to know them. Through them I managed to somewhat keep up with technology, and have some understanding about what goes on in the media. I don't feel as old and out of touch as some of my peer group. There are tremendous advantages to being surrounded by young people. I forget that I am seventy-six, and because I rarely look in the mirror I think I am ageless. Sometimes when passing the mirror on the dresser in my bedroom, I almost yell out, *"Help! There is some old woman in my bedroom!"* It is a good thing to accept aging, after all, it happens to everybody, if you are lucky enough to live for a long time. Yes, I was beautiful once, but age too has incredible advantages. Suddenly, you are no longer a woman, dealing with sexism, unwanted advances, being treated like a dumb blonde. You become a person. Somehow, an older person has more respect and credibility. People see you for who you are, not for your looks. Most people have a grandmother, so even policemen are less likely to give you a speeding ticket. You can go to the movies alone, without getting hit on. You can walk down a dangerous street because even criminals have grandmothers. They too are less likely to attack an old woman. It is a new experience to be invisible. People don't notice an old woman. You become part of the landscape. They say you get wisdom as you age, it is true. But, then again, have you ever seen someone whistle at your wisdom?

Running this theatre company has been my full time job. After our directors recruit the actors, we need to check references, and issue contracts. When the actors for the season are due to arrive they need to be picked up at airports and bus stations. Most of them live far and few of them drive.

Sleeping quarters need to be cleaned and made ready. Bedding has to be made available and heating, or in summer, cooling fans. Such appliances need to be checked and turned on before people get here. I do all the cooking, everyday, sometimes for up to twenty people, depending on how many tours we are sending out for the season. We grow a lot of produce in the summer. I preserve and freeze a lot of it. I cook large aluminum containers of food for the freezer, and usually have at least twenty frozen meals ready before a new group arrives.

I keep a large stock of staples, such as flour, sugar, coffee, condiments, pasta, oil, and cleaning supplies. When the nearest supermarket is twenty miles away it requires a fair amount of planning. I pride myself for hardly ever running out of something I need to prepare a meal. Shopping for this amount of people is also quite an expedition. I do this at least once a week.

We supply the actors' food for breakfast, lunch, and a cooked dinner usually followed by a homemade desert. I also have to take into account food allergies and other dietary needs. All this takes a lot of work, but food for me, is a form of nurturing, tradition, and love. I never turn away anyone from my table. Over the years I have seen a lot of changes in young actors' eating habits. More and more, are vegetarian. A lot don't eat red meat and most are health conscious. I am delighted when people love what I cook and the more they like it, the harder I try to please them. Normally, a lot of these young people have limited funds so they love interesting and sometimes different culinary experiences. I cook, and the actors have an evening schedule, where two of them clean the kitchen after dinner.

I am in charge of designing and supervising the sewing of all the costumes, organize the props, and fit each actor with costumes. I also make sure the props are good and the wigs fit properly. During rehearsals, there are lots of costume details to adjust and alter, and for this, sometimes I do have help. When we used to have ten or more two man teams, each rehearsing two plays, it was twenty separate sets of costumes. After losing my mother, I had some wonderful helpers, the problem is that this work is seasonal and I can't hire somebody fulltime. The sets consist of canvas covered flats, with a curtain in the middle and a painted drop on either side depicting scenes relevant to each play. These were always painted by my dear friend here in Barnstead, the immensely talented Sandy Burt. No one else ever measured up to her!

After a three week rehearsal the actors pack the flats, drops, props and costumes in mini vans, and fan out over the contiguous forty-eight states. The company provides a salary and everything else on the road, except food. There is an average of two shows a day, sometimes in two close but different locations. We perform in schools, theatres, and libraries for K-through eighth grades. In the last few years, school budgets have been cut drastically and of course it is always the "Arts" that are first to go. Somehow nurturing the soul takes a backseat to sports. Having given up teaching about God in schools, we now worship sports instead. We worship the "Ball" like sun worshippers. The amount of money spent on arts is but a tiny fraction of what people spend on sports. Parents support sports because a lot of them watch sports and expect their little Johnny to play in the big league, and earn millions. This is mathematically less likely than winning the lottery!

Not that long ago we used to perform three thousand shows a year. We now perform only about a thousand. I still feel we make a difference in the lives of so many children.

The biggest success and innovation was when we started the "Shakespeare for Kid" series. No one has attempted tackling Shakespeare for the younger kids. They never even introduce Shakespeare before high school. This was a great and successful time, until most theatre companies for kids started copying us, and now everybody is doing Shakespeare; but we were the first!

Our performances are interactive and some of the children get to act and participate on stage for a short time. They love it! We sometimes get very funny letters. One of our Shakespeare plays has scenes from Romeo and Juliet, and our writer very cleverly managed to introduce the suicide scene without frightening the children. In the play, the actor dressed as Shakespeare is trying to teach the actress how to "die" on stage. She overacts and he decides to call up a couple of volunteers to show her how to do it properly. Much hamming and merriment ensues, and the kids take the suicide scene very naturally. We once got a letter: "Dear Hampstead Players, thank you for letting me die!" Sometimes children sent illustrations and little stories, but all the letters prove that you can never underestimate the intelligence and comprehension of kids. During thirty years we have performed for and influenced thousands of children. A few years ago, one of our directors was on a flight to the West Coast. As we tend to do on long flights, he started talking to the young man in the next seat. The young man happened to be an actor and when asked why he chose this profession, he answered:" When I was in grade school, a traveling theatre company came and performed a play at my school, and I was smitten. They were called something like "Hampstead..." and they were just great! I get goose bumps every time I tell this story. It was one of our high points.

Like all occupations, we also have low points. Our actors drove up to what they thought was the school (which was attached to a church) and jumping out of the van shouted a greeting to the crowd, "Where would you like us to entertain you, today?" Unfortunately, the crowd was there waiting for a funeral service."

Once our actors showed up for an afternoon performance at a town in New York, only to find out a town by the same name, also in New York, was expecting them instead, at the same time, two hours away! We had very few disasters such as these, most of our shows are on time and very successful and these days everyone has GPS.

Because our shows consist of only two actors, they each play several different characters, using a variety of costumes and voice changes. The most frequent comments in letters sent to us, are the disbelief, that there were really only two actors playing so many characters.

Some of our actors stay with us, the longest was seven years, others come for a season and return again after a few years, some move on and we don't see them again. We have an alumni page and I love to hear from our kids.

Over the years there were five weddings, between young people who met during their work with us. I always feel I should be the one giving them away. Thankfully, we have never had a serious car accident among our teams, and other than minor colds and food related problems, our actors have been resilient and healthy. It is a tremendous responsibility to send young people driving thousands of miles all over the country. I am the quintessential "Jewish mother" and spend hours checking for weather problems and making sure the actors are safe and sound. It is a very large family with all its problems, but I get a lot of joy out of it.

My enthusiasm has remained constant, but the years have made it more difficult for me to keep up with the work.

X.
SPEAKER

When my granddaughter Simone was in eighth grade at her school in Manchester, New Hampshire, she talked to school friends about the Holocaust and realized that her classmates knew nothing about it! Ten years ago it had not been taught in most schools. She organized with her teachers to have me come and speak to her class. I had never done this before and I was concerned about how it would go. I did no preparation ahead of time and simply started telling my family's story. At first the kids were a fidgety group, bored, looking around—not rude, but pretty disinterested.

As I started speaking, there was a gradual change. Within ten minutes I had their complete attention. I started by telling them why I decided to speak. There are fewer and fewer survivors and witnesses alive to inform young people as time passes. I had not been in a concentration camp. The handful of people who had survived in my town are mostly dead now. The child survivors are those who were hidden by people, who took pity on them and tried to do the right thing, usually at great peril to themselves.

I told my audience about Nagyvarad, my home town, the cultured peaceful, calm, prosperous place. I described the libraries, the Opera house, the cinemas, the parks and swimming pools, and the long shaded walks by the river which ran through town. I talked about my mother—a dressmaker, employing forty girls with clients coming from all over to have her make beautiful garments. I spoke about my Daddy who owned a wholesale fish business. They were wealthy, traveled all over Europe. We had maids, a cook, a housekeeper, and a governess. We did not have a car, but most people didn't, and when we needed to somewhere we hired a horse drawn carriage.

I talked about my love for Daddy who was always kind and patient, who never yelled and always had some little surprise for me in his pocket when he came home. I described how I would sit on his lap on the balcony, and how he would teach me the names of all the stars. I told them about the complete love and security I felt in his arms. He was the center of my universe.

Daddy always gave me money to give to the poor and explained that they were people just like us, who were not lucky to have our privileges. I was not supposed to judge or feel that I was any better than a poor beggar.

I talked about my little friend Istvanka, who had a sculpture of his head on his parents' mantelpiece. I spoke about how I envied Istvanka for this, but how I loved the beautiful little boy with the blue eyes and curly golden hair.

Mother, who converted to Judaism, would light candles on Friday nights and wave her hands over the flames, saying things in a language I didn't understand and I thought she was doing magic.

I told them about my golden, privileged, childhood—the beloved, spoiled little princess I was, the apple of my beloved Daddy's eye, the secure loving, beautiful world I lived in. I talked about my parents not wanting to deprive me of the festivities and having a huge Christmas tree every year with every conceivable toy and presents underneath it. I told them about the little candles that set the tree on fire every year and the bucket of water that stood by to put it out, and how when our maid took me to see the nativity display at the local church, I stole baby Jesus. It was found under my coat when we got home.

After this incident my parents decided that they needed to rein in their wild four-and-a-half year old child. The solution was *"Fraulein"* a tall skinny sour Austrian German governess who was to make a lady of me. I hated Fraulein, but she did teach me to speak, read, and write German in only a few months. I was no longer allowed to play with the children on the street and was only to mix with suitable children from "good "families.

I told them how I had to sleep in curlers and have my hair beautifully combed every morning. I wore white stockings and patent leather shoes and was paraded every morning in front of my parents to show how a little girl from a "good family" had to look. I was taken to elegant birthday parties to children's houses from "good families." I wore blue velvet dresses with white lace collars, and I was never, never, allowed outside without white gloves. I was allowed to play with Istvanka only because he was from the right class.

I complained to my parents about Fraulein but they felt it was the right thing to educate me properly. They meant well.

They decided I should also learn about being Jewish so they sent me two mornings a week to a Jewish Kindergarten, where I learned to sing little songs in Hebrew and played with the other children. There were fifty-two children. Istvanka was there too.

When my father's relatives came for a meal we had to put together two long tables, for the twenty-seven extra people. They were big, loud, happy meals. I had so many aunts, uncles, and cousins. They were such wonderful happy times.

Then slowly things started to change. People stopped talking when I came into the room. I often found my mother crying, people who had always there, started to leave. Everyone was sad and short tempered, even Daddy stopped laughing. What I, as a child, didn't know was that new anti-Jewish laws were very scary. First, Jews couldn't go to university. Next, they could not attend high school, and then they were only allowed to go to a Jewish school. Maids younger than forty-five were not allowed to work for Jews. Jewish doctors were not allowed to treat Christians, and Jews were not allowed to sit on certain park benches or go to the public swimming pool.

Fraulein left suddenly, which made me very happy, but I missed the maids and some of my mother's dressmakers. When I questioned the grownups, I was told not to worry, everything would be all right. But it wasn't.

I recounted how my mother made me a beautiful shiny gold star and sewed it on my blue coat. I loved the pretty shiny star and proudly walked down the street with mother to buy some pastries. A man came opposite us, stepped in front of me, and stared at my star. I looked up at him expecting him to say what a beautiful star it was. He simply spat in my face, the spit running down onto my shiny star. I couldn't understand why the man hated stars. It did not occur to me it was me he hated. I looked up at my mother expecting her to yell at the man. Instead, she grabbed me and started pulling me quickly towards our house. I was shocked that my mother was not protecting me.

The Hungarian Nazi authorities cordoned off a few city blocks and placed a high barbed wire fence around it. Jews were to pack one suitcase each. The police came and moved them all into this area. They called it the Ghetto. *"Ghetto"* had been the name of an old foundry in Venice, the only place where in the Middle Ages Italian Jews were allowed to live. They were allowed out during the day, but after dark they were forbidden to be anywhere but in the Ghetto. My whole Jewish family was taken to the Ghetto and even Istvanka was gone. Some of the families were taken so suddenly that they had no time to make arrangement for their pets. Poor, scared, hungry dogs were roaming the streets. Then the dog catcher came and took them all away.

I told the children that some people converted to Catholicism thinking they would be able to stay out of the Ghetto. I was not supposed to be in the room, but I hid behind the sofa, when a priest came to convert my father. Mother had bribed someone and smuggled Daddy out to meet the priest. Daddy was kneeling with tears running down his face, saying prayers. Converting didn't help. He had to go back to the ghetto.

I remember him leaving. My parents were standing next to a table holding each other, crying. I climbed onto the table and wormed my way between them. Because they cried, I started crying too. This was the last time I saw my father.

My mother hid me in the backroom of our house. I had to be silent and I was not allowed to show my face, because being half-Jewish, I too was supposed to be in the Ghetto.

I told the children about Erzsebet, the peasant woman who used to sell us milk from her farm. She had been a poor orphan and years ago, my mother made her the gift of a beautiful wedding dress. Erzsebet never forgot it. When she heard they were rounding up the Jews, she came to see my mother and told her she would hide me on her farm. Mother came to tell me I was going on a great adventure, to a farm where there were animals and I would have great fun. I hopped up on the bench in her cart and we drove to the farm. To my surprise, Erzsebet did not take me into her house but took me to the barn. There were two stalls, one for the cow and one for the horse with a hayloft above it. She took me to the loft and told me I had to stay there and hide because people were trying to kill me. The concept of death is alien to a child and I could not imagine why anyone would want to hurt me. I was a good girl after all.

A record from a database maintained in Jerusalem of my father **Erno Rubin's** demise in a Concentration Camp in 1944.

Erzsebet brought me food and blankets and showed me how to burrow in the hay and hide in case anyone came up the stairs to look for me. I cried for a long time. I cried for my mother and my daddy and I was scared of the big spiders and the dark. I cried myself to sleep for a few days and slowly I stopped crying.

Sometimes, late at night, Erzsebet took me to her house to wash me and I got to play with her dog. One early morning I woke to a commotion in front of the barn and looked through a crack in the wood to see what was going on. There were three soldiers in green uniforms and hats with big black rooster feathers, pushing and slapping Erzsebet, yelling, "Where is the half-breed bastard Jew?"

She told them to go look in her house. After searching the house, they had the bright idea to check out the barn. They stuck bayonets on their rifles and started up the stairs to the attic. I did what she taught me and I buried myself under the hay where the roof and the floor of the attic met. I made myself very small and held my breath. The soldiers started stabbing the hay to see if anyone was hiding. One of the bayonets stuck in the floor an inch from my cheek. I still remember the "twang" it made as the soldier pulled it free. I grew up that day. I knew what it meant that someone wants to kill me.

One of my mother's employees told the police that I was hidden and they had arrested mother. She was tortured but never told them where I was hidden, and never told me what they did to her. She said it was too humiliating.

She managed to bribe someone to smuggle daddy out of the Ghetto once again. He was going to cross the border into Romania where they were not deporting the Jews. Before his journey, he wanted to see me and tell me he was going away again. He wanted to reassure me he would be back. He walked, late at night, all the way to the village. They caught him on the road and he was put on the train Auschwitz the next day. I never saw him again.

I told the children how happy I was when the Russians started invading. My mother came and took me home. The bombs were falling and we had to stay in the basement most of the time. There was not much to eat, but I didn't have to hide anymore and I was with my mother. We ate potatoes and more potatoes. After a while we stopped going to the shelter in the basement and watched the war from the window. A poor skinny horse was pulling a cart with someone's pathetic belongings and it simply collapsed in front of the house. The carter whipped it to get it up but the poor animal had died. Within minutes women came with knives and bowls and cut up the horse. They pulled off the skin cut off bits of meat still warm and steaming. In no time at all the meat was gone. Soon they were gathering the bones to make soup. This was when we all ate horsemeat. We were so terribly hungry.

The battle was raging within sight. The Russian soldiers came across the frozen river in waves, linking arms and singing. As they approached they were mowed down by machine guns. But they kept coming in waves climbing over the dead still linking arms, still singing. I am sure they were drunk because nobody is this brave. The bodies were piling up and finally as another group climbed over the dead, arms linked, singing, the machine guns stopped and we were under Russian occupation.

The Russians were molesting women but they generally liked children and left them alone. My mother, in her take charge way, decided to go and see the new commander. She blackened her teeth, rubbed soot on her face, stuck a pillow under her dress to look like a hunchback, covered her hair with a scarf, put on an old dress and bent over, shuffling with a cane. To her amazement the Russian commander was a young woman. By this time the Russians lost so many soldiers they were promoting women and very young soldiers. My mother told the commander through an interpreter to come to her house and she would make her a beautiful dress. When she came, as usual, I hid and watched what happened. Mother made her throw away the horrible old fashioned bra and made her a beautiful dress from one of the drapes. She also fixed her hair and the commander looked really pretty. After this, not only did other female soldiers come for dresses, but we had food. We got butter, sugar, eggs, meat, apples, and even chocolate. We also had a guard outside our house so no one would bother us.

This is when Ivan came into my life. Ivan was a captain, barely seventeen, with an adjutant, an older, fat, happy man who constantly played his accordion and sang. They drank a lot too. They drank cologne, alcohol, meths, anything they could get their hands on. They were drunk most of the time, but they were happy drunks. They were very nice to me. I sang with them and they played games with me.

One day Ivan brought us a whole goose liver, which was a great delicacy, even before the war. There were traces of blood on it so he decided to wash it in the toilet. He pulled the chain , the liver disappeared so Ivan shot the toilet. They used the moldings around the ceiling for target practice, and when it got too cold, they broke up antique furniture and used it to heat the rooms. But I did love Ivan. He said he would come back when I was seventeen and marry me. He was sent somewhere and disappeared into the fog of war, the poor boy.

Soon survivors from the liberated concentration camps started arriving home to look for any surviving members of their families. My mother and I walked to the train station every evening. We stood on the platform, holding my daddy's picture and asking if anyone had seen him?. I was sure he would be on the train. After all, my big strong Daddy would never leave me. Nobody knew him, and we walked back home crying. I was scared of the people who got off the trains. They were like ghosts, thin, in rags, with no hair. I couldn't tell, if they were men or women. Mother started taking some of them home with us. She gave them baths and clothes. As usual, I hid and listened to their horrible stories from the camps. I still sometimes have nightmares, remembering.

One evening, at the train station, a man came up to my mother. At first, she did not recognize him. He used to be the owner of the most elegant hotel and casino in town. My parents used to play cards there every week. He told us not to wait for Daddy because he was not coming back. He was dead. He didn't tell us how, just that he saw him and he was dead.

My Father

Mother took him home, gave him some clothes and he went to see his family's housekeeper with whom they left everything for safekeeping. He knocked on the door and the woman opened it wearing his wife's dress. There was a shocked look on her face. "So they didn't kill you? Anyway the Russians took everything," she said, slamming the door in his face. The poor man went to Romania to visit his mother who also didn't recognize him when he stood at her door.

The man came back to live with us. Somehow out of two broken remnants we were able to make a new family. He became my stepfather. When I grew up he told me how my father died. Daddy and a friend stole a piece of bread. They were caught and the SS commander decided to make an example of them. They stripped them naked, beat them with whips and metal bars and put each of the into a dog cage. They were placed in the middle of the parade ground where the prisoners had to line up every morning to be counted. It was very cold, and it took my Daddy two nights and a day to die in agony.

My stepfather also told me that after three days of terrible inhuman suffering in a cattle car he and his family arrived in Auschwitz. They stood on the platform where Dr. Mengele, who was in charge of selection, sent his wife and eleven-year-old daughter to the left. He was shuffled off to the right. When he saw his family disappearing in the distance, he asked one of the guards, "Where are they going?" "There," said the guard simply pointing to the smoking crematorium chimney.

I showed them a picture of the little girl, Ditta, and told them that when I die, nobody will remember her. I asked them not to forget, so that her life would matter. I talked about my sorrow for the extinguished potential, all the scientists, writers, doctors, artists, musicians and other brilliant people who were killed, the potential of the generations who would have come after them, so much good wasted, by murderous fanatic psychopaths.

Much later, in America, when my stepfather had Alzheimer and was dying he called me Ditta. I didn't correct him. I let him believe he was holding the hand of his beloved little girl.

It took me fifty years to get over hate, but it is not for me to forgive someone else's death. I have

Dita

sorrow now, but not hate, and I have a lot of love in my heart. When your heart is full of hatred there is no room for anything else. I am not a victim, because if I felt I was a victim they would have won. I am a survivor. I have four sons and every time I gave birth to a Jewish child, I felt I was giving the finger to Hitler. I have four granddaughters, we are a multi-cultural family. We have family members who are half African American, Mexican, German, and Chinese and they are all beautiful. I am happy.

So now I need to speak for the dead who cannot speak. I think ten percent of people are really good, ten percent are bad, and the rest are sheep. So if you need to follow a shepherd make sure you choose a good one and not one who is evil. It is so much harder to be good, because you actively have to try and help. It is much easier to follow evil blindly, but being bad , does not make you happy, unless you are a psychopath. If you see evil you have to get involved. If you do not, it is as bad as being an active perpetrator. Be counted and stand up, try to make a difference.

Do not look away when somebody is persecuted or bullied. One act of kindness and tolerance each day can change your world.

I told them about Pastor Niemoller who wrote: "When they came for the trade unionist I didn't speak up because I was not one of them, when they came for the communists I didn't speak up because I was not a communist, when they came for the Jews I didn't speak up because I was not a Jew, and when they came for me there was no one left to speak up."

There is genocide going on every day, somewhere in our world today. The only thing you can do is stand up and be counted. It is your world and it will be what you make of it, every one of you. Educate people against prejudice, and bullying, and respect everyone, no matter how different they are to you. It is your world, fight to make it wonderful!

When I finished speaking, there was stunned silence and then the kids erupted into clapping and cheering. I opened it up for questions, which seemed to go on for a long time. One boy told us that he saw his mother and sister raped in Bosnia. Another child from Africa told us she was found roaming on the streets in Somalia and she had no idea who she was before she was adopted into her new family here in the United States. So much pain, and yet so much hope and open willingness to engage. They lined up and started hugging and kissing me and thanking me for speaking. I could not believe the deep connection I had with these wonderful young people.

I realized this was to be the reason for my life from now on—to speak and try to make a difference, to inform, tell my story, and connect with kids who may have studied about the Holocaust, but history is cold and unconnected to their reality today.

I lost count of how many places I have spoken at in the last few years. I have spoken at universities, theatres, churches, libraries, synagogues, Masonic Lodges, High schools, Rotary Clubs and many middle schools. My story seems to affect most audiences, but my favorite group to speak to, remain the eighth graders, when children are on the cusp of becoming adults. They are half angels and half devils. If I can reach the angels in them it makes an enormous difference to what they may become. I love these children, their defensive bravado and swagger, their carapace of *"cool,"* their open minds, their compassion, and ability to embrace an idea of tolerance and acceptance. I have spent fifteen years on our town's school board, and I think education is the most important thing in a child's life and future. We should invest much, much more, in these precious treasures, our children. Most genocides and atrocities have been perpetrated by ignorance, fear, hatred, and prejudice. The only way is **education**, because we can teach tolerance by connecting to the souls of these young people. I am very optimistic about this new generation growing up now. They are far more open-minded and aware that there is a world out there and we are all part of it.

The questions the children ask after my talks, open a whole new world for me. Their world, their understanding of it, trying to define themselves and find their individual space in it. I receive many letters, all very loving and appreciative, but some stand out.

One girl told me about being bullied in school. I got in touch with her teachers who had no idea this had been going on behind the scene, she had not been able to confide in anyone before. Another girl whose parents had just divorced, realized that her life was still really good because she still had both her parents, both alive and she felt my story made her appreciate her own life. A boy, who could not reconcile his two races and decide which to embrace, realized it was okay to be different. You don't have to be black or white but you can be a unique individual.

One girl decided to become a pediatric oncologist to help suffering children and another girl wrote that she feels she has to make a difference in the world in some capacity when she grows up. One little girl wrote that she will now make her dream come true and become a female welder! A boy wrote that he wants to change the world but doesn't know how, where to begin? Many, many, children write: "I will not be a sheep." Some of them call me brave for being able to stand in front of many people and talk about painful memories. In the beginning it was difficult, but now, all the love and compassion I feel coming back to me after I speak, makes me happy. It heals me, and energizes me, makes me hopeful and optimistic, that if these young people can retain the compassion and caring they show me, it will be a better world.

My sons call me terminally optimistic. It is true. I am a survivor, not a victim and we can change things and make the world a better place...

I have become involved with the wonderful faculty of the Cohen Center for Genocide and Holocaust Studies at Keene State College, in New Hampshire. Although many colleges offer holocaust studies, Keene is the only college offering a degree in the subject. What is also unique, the members of this wonderful, erudite and dedicated faculty are not Jewish. Most of them are Theologians and Christians. They are what true Christians should be. I had the privilege to sit in on some of their lectures, and their knowledge of the history, politics and sociology during Nazism is amazing. I could spend the rest of my life listening to them, there is so much to learn. I am also very impressed with the students who attend this great institution. For young people to embark on acquiring a degree in holocaust studies takes enormous dedication and courage. In our world today, with the cost of education, and the difficulty in getting a well paying job to eventually pay for it are great obstacles. Yet year after year the students come because somewhere their souls were touched by the horrors of the past and they want to make a difference. When I questioned some of them why, they invariably talked about being exposed to history during school. Most of these students are not Jewish who may have been touched by family history, they were all educated and felt the need to do something about the wrongs in our world.

So I will keep speaking for the rest of my life, for Daddy, Ditta, Istvanka, and the millions of who cannot speak anymore.

Now the circle is closed.

THE END

THANK YOUS

I owe so many thanks to so many, for my life, my friendships and support.

First I want to thank Yoram Matmor who gave me wings.

To, Tom White, my mentor and friend who saw the potential in my story to heal, and try to bring change through speaking to young people. Through the Cohen Center at Keene State College, I have met amazing human beings whose purpose in life is to bring tolerance and understanding into this troubled world. I will always be grateful.

To my editor, Anura Gurugé, without whose friendship, wisdom, patience and input this book would not have been finished.

To my wonderful husband of many years, Gordon, for his unending tolerance, support, patience and kindness.

To my dear friend, Karen Schacht, who encouraged me, and nagged me to finish writing. Her faith in the importance of my story, led me to finally find the true meaning in my life, speaking, and writing.

To my family who put up with me all these years and my wonderful young actors and actresses who kept me from ageing, gracefully or disgracefully, by treating me like one of them.

I love all of you.

Kati Preston
Barnstead, New Hampshire
January 2016